The Art of Teaching

A central dilemma for teachers is finding ways to deal with the multiple perspectives and demands of pupils, parents, school management and external forces.

The Art of Teaching explores the tension between teaching and learning that all teachers face. Presenting a series of insights into the art of teaching from the perspectives of those individuals most closely involved in the schooling process, the book explores pupil voice in schools and experiences of teaching and learning from the pupil viewpoint. Providing an opportunity for self-reflection, the book also examines teachers' relationships with parents, external agencies and their attitudes towards pupils.

Subjects covered include:

- what pupils think of teachers;
- teachers' views of themselves and self-reflection;
- school hierarchies and the ethos of inspection;
- using pupil insights to inform learning strategies.

Essential reading for all teachers and students, this book offers a unique insight into school relationships and structures, giving readers an awareness of what is like to be a teacher.

Cedric Cullingford was formerly Professor of Education at the University of Huddersfield. His many books include *The Causes of Exclusion* (Routledge) and *How Pupils Cope with School* (Cambridge Scholar's Press).

The Art of Teaching

Experiences of schools

Cedric Cullingford

Routledge
Taylor & Francis Group

LONDON AND NEW YORK

First published 2010
by Routledge
2 Park Square, Milton Park, Abingdon, Oxon OX14 4RN

Simultaneously published in the USA and Canada
by Routledge
270 Madison Avenue, New York, NY 10016

Routledge is an imprint of the Taylor & Francis Group, an informa business

© 2010 Cedric Cullingford

Typeset in Bembo by
HWA Text and Data Management, London
Printed and bound in Great Britain by
CPI Antony Rowe, Chippenham, Wiltshire

British Library Cataloguing in Publication Data
A catalogue record for this book is available from the British Library

Library of Congress Cataloging in Publication Data
Cullingford, Cedric.
   The art of teaching : experiences of school / Cedric Cullingford.
      p. cm.
   1. Teaching. 2. Teachers – Professional relationships. I. Title.
   LB1025.3.C783 2009
   371.102–dc22   2009005889

ISBN 10: 0–415–49250–5 (hbk)
ISBN 10: 0–415–49251–3 (pbk)

ISBN 13: 978–0–415–49250–8 (hbk)
ISBN 13: 978–0–415–49251–5 (pbk)

For Sir Tim Brighouse: the supporter of teachers

Contents

Preface

This book is a celebration of learning. It is also a consolation to teachers.

Teachers need constantly to be reminded about the pleasures and necessities of learning. Whilst hunger and thirst might be more immediate, the desire to learn is the starting point of human life. Just as we are aware of the unique power of language, we must also recognise the deep-seated human desire to learn; it is something innate but not immutable, something fragile as well as resilient.

Nothing gives more real joy than the pleasures of learning. These come at a variety of different levels. Learning can be something simply done for its own sake but it always has some kind of consequence. It can include distractions, the 'chewing-gum' of the mind, like crossword puzzles or Sudoku. It can consist of the accumulation of facts, lists and statistics. It can be expressed in experiences, for sport is its own kind of learning. It can be a matter of defining things exactly, making refined distinctions, and it can also be the formulation of opinions, with all their emotional drive.

Learning is ultimately a matter of understanding. This can be applied to ourselves and other people, to society and the environment. The significance of learning is that it always takes place, even if it is learning not to think or not to care. Learning always takes place but it can be destructive; it is never simply the acquisition of knowledge.

This book is about and for teachers, and therefore has as its central theme the importance of learning. Why? Where do teachers come into it?

There are three reasons for emphasising learning:

- The first is that teaching can only be experienced and understood as a means of fostering learning in others. The 'delivery of the curriculum', that telling political phase, misses the point entirely.
- The second is that teachers suffer if they themselves do not learn and enjoy learning. Teachers have a far greater effect by demonstrating their own love of learning than by any other means.
- The third is that teachers are necessary from the learner's point of view; all people need others to act as teachers. This is why there are so many definitions of teachers, from guides to coaches to mentors.

The main reason for concentrating on learning is the fact (which experienced teachers realise and which is worth constant repetition) that people love to learn and resent being taught. The subtlety of teaching rests on this fact.

There is another reason for concentrating on learning, and that is that the education system is built on quite different principles. Teachers are in a difficult position. This has been exacerbated by the regime of inspection and the National Curriculum, so that all teachers are now aware of this, but teachers have always been in an awkward spot, between the demands of the State and the needs of their pupils.

The research that informs this book is not just derived from teachers but from the experience of pupils. If we listen to what pupils say, then it will be clear that there is something structurally wrong with the way the system operates – and there always has been. The motivation for schooling has nearly always been equivocal. The wealth of historical literature reveals how schools have been used for all kinds of purposes – for the development of skills for trade and industry, for the acquisition of attitudes to command, for making up for the deficiencies of parents and the community, for keeping the young occupied – but there has never been a central emphasis on pupils' learning needs, for their own sake.

The system of education, as it has evolved, based on a factory model of an old fashioned kind, of input and outcomes, of instrumental measurement and competition, has never been suited to the pupils that are supposed to be its reason for existence. The atavistic assumptions that are not only deeply inbred but passed on unquestioned from generation to generation are based on simple models of progressive development, starting with a baseline of deficiency. The only deficiencies that young children have are of knowledge and conventions, not of intellect, and it is this on which the education system is mistakenly dependent.

Teaching is a subtle and delicate art and the prowess displayed by teachers should never be underestimated. But teaching has become associated with the control and command of children, with discipline and authority. The fact that this is so, and that new teachers are most concerned with coping with this unnatural situation, says a great deal more about the education system than it does about teaching. There is something absurd about the fact that reluctant young people have to be coerced into learning, but this is what the system has become and the pupils resent this deeply. To reduce education to the smothering of individuals with meaningless facts on which they will be tested, and to battles of will in which all kinds of psychological tricks are used, is essentially absurd.

This absurdity, however, is what teachers face. The ideal clashes against reality. This book is concerned with reality so that it deals with both the ideal and the actual. It also reveals the views of the pupils who are far more critical of the system than those who run it and who see the absurdities while either adapting or submitting to them. The tone might sound at times rather negative, but this comes about because teachers need to know the reality, and the more they do so the more they can retain the ideals that we all share.

The book is designed to be a consolation for teachers in difficult circumstances. By exploring the defects, it reminds us of the best of teaching. By acknowledging the problems it celebrates the real achievement of teachers.

The true art of teaching lies in character and responsiveness. It is the ability to listen and take others seriously, with politeness but without judgement, with curiosity but without intrusiveness, and with the ability to listen without aching to talk about oneself.

The teacher is the greatest of resources – not of knowledge but of sharing the desire to explore it. The teacher is the person willing to be turned to, to explore ideas in an iterative fashion. The teacher is a Socratic philosopher who does not pretend to lay down the law but who pursues all the complexities of meaning, interpretations and feeling.

When pupils remember the teachers who have influenced them it is always for two reasons. The first is the character, the interesting personality, willing to learn and to have ideas, with their own interests and developing curiosity. The second is the fact that the teacher takes them as individuals at face value; they listen and they are interested in receiving ideas rather than simply presenting them.

This picture of the teacher contrasts with the demands made by almost all formal systems of education – a system where information is forced on what are assumed to be reluctant inmates.

The teacher is someone with a particular expertise. It does not matter what this is. It can be simply the awareness of other people, or manifest integrity. In the views of the pupils the teacher is someone special, not because they assume a role but because they can be a help.

A teacher simply exhibits civilised values. This might sound an old fashioned concept, but it still suggests that the importance lies in character and not simply in performance. Pupils can be merciless to those who are false to themselves and who rely on the power of their effect on others, for approval or obedience.

The ideal teacher is surrounded, and sometimes diminished, by the quite contrary expectations of delivery and performance. This explains all the emphasis that is placed on 'leadership' as if this were simply a type of checklist of commands and accountability. This arid view of managerialism stems from the culture of government in which each person is competing to demonstrate his or her own prowess against that of others. The culture of government – adversarial, uncollegial, obsessed by target setting, overwhelmed by repetitive manifestos and policy initiatives – affects the way that schools are run.

This quite different attitude towards the way that the world should be organised has become deeply embedded in the consciousness of those who have power, but it is equally as instinctively dismissed by those who are involved in learning. The two cultures simply do not mix. This is why teachers, real teachers, those who do not adapt to managerialism, feel essentially uncomfortable. The task that they carry out is not understood, and therefore despised. If things do not work it is teachers who are blamed, as if the instrumental designs of policy were such that it should be easy to fulfil.

The fact that there has always been a tension between the ethos of the education system and the nature of learning is far more significant than the present political implications. To understand the difficulties teachers face in terms of political bickering does not help them. To understand, teachers need to know how deep rooted the dilemmas are.

The reality, as well as the ideal, on which this book is based is one that has long been with us even if we are naturally more conscious of how it affects the present time. Teachers can survive, can help, can do great things, and can fulfil themselves by understanding and reflecting on the nature of their positions. This might seem uncomfortable and sometimes it will be salutary, especially when hearing the points of view of their pupils. But in the end it will be more than a consolation.

Teachers need all the support they can get, because as individuals they can be exposed and blamed and criticised. Their role is, however, far more collective on the one hand and individual on the other. If we centre on the facts of learning then we see how many people are involved in supporting, and helping and cajoling. In this the teachers are part of a collective which includes many people not officially 'teachers'. In this framework, teachers make a great deal of difference as individuals. It is the inadvertent that counts, the integrity, the enthusiasm that is suddenly noticed and has an influence of enormous consequences. The teacher will not necessarily be aware of this; indeed, if he or she desperately tries to affect it, there will be nothing but trouble.

The emphasis is on the pupils' learning. Can they therefore learn without being taught in some way or other? The answer is an emphatic no. There might be a solipsistic desire to suggest that each person is self-made, without any help from anyone else, and we often hear this arrogant statement about self-help being made as if the individual asserting it were completely unaware of the subtlety and pervasiveness of influence. It might be an interesting psychological ploy, but it is simply not true. Learning is always a social activity and learned, like language, in a specific context. It is vulnerable to all kinds of influences and no one is more likely to be affected by others than those who assume that they are self-made.

Pupils also need saving from the worst influences of social attitudes, the prevailing norms of the time. We need to understand how a society, like Nazi Germany, can become embroiled in a hideous collective mood. Teachers should be those who emphasise the importance of individuality rather than collective goals and attitudes. Pupils need guidance, not in the given curriculum, but to learn to think for themselves.

In this emphasis on learning, the idea of a teacher becomes something different and more cultural, not simply a conveyor of knowledge but an example and an influence. The idea of a teacher is even more ambiguous in that it is a matter both of form and of status.

How does one distinguish between the teacher and the assistant? Is there a difference between management and support, or between dealing with a large class and responding to individuals? How does one make a distinction between the teacher and the lecturer? Is it a matter of 'delivering' knowledge, which can be recovered or ignored, as opposed to nurturing individual learning?

What are the differences between teachers and mentors, or between teachers and coaches? We all accept the difference between the command and status of those in control of a mass of pupils, and those who work with individuals. But the best teaching is also individual; a personal interpretation of what can be learned. Our habit of associating teachers with a certain manner, with discipline and command, or in the worst memories, of shouting and punishing, points to a strongly held attitude which might be a mere image or symbol but is a collective belief at the same time. Teachers have been pressed into the images of self-parody.

The idea of this book is to explore, from the pupils' and the teachers' points of view, what it is like to teach, when one reflects on it. Often teachers find their roles difficult, and this book is an attempt to explain why. It does not come up with easy answers but it should be more than a consolation to understand why there are ambiguities and what to do about it. One thing that cannot be done is immediately to change the education system, even if it is wrong. But one day this will come about. When it does it will be because teachers, supported by parents, prevail, and because the research evidence will then be heard. Meanwhile, teachers have to know that the problems are not their fault. The only blame that could be laid against them collectively is that they are inadvertently propping up a failed system. In the middle of all these policies and the constant strictures, teachers do more good than they imagine.

I gratefully thank the many teachers and pupils who have talked so honestly and constructively about their experiences, and those who have helped, even if inadvertently, like Bob Butroyd, Judy Gill, Rod Robertson, Catherine Scott, Amanda Snelling and Gill Trorey.

The children

There was once a book, fashionable at the time, which listed a whole series of dilemmas. This was to make an academic theory of all the different problems of being a teacher, and there were plenty from which to choose. For us as teachers, however, although there are many tensions and conflicts, it does not feel that there are theoretical dilemmas that need to be addressed one by one. Instead, the experience of teaching is an activity of constant and instant decision-making, the kind of chaotic circumstances that make theoretical positioning seem absurd and which draw attention to the experience, the latent knowledge and the instinctive intelligence that teachers bring to bear. With such pressure it seems difficult to be theoretical, but thinking about what we do is a necessity for teachers and a way to cope.

To stand back and think of a number of different dilemmas as if they were at the same level is all very well but the tension is far more immediate and far more real. Beneath the busiest activities teachers experience a number of very real tensions and conflicts between different forces and different influences. There is a constant need to resolve these by being aware of them.

Some of the tensions that teachers face are obvious. They are to do with the result of government policies and all the contradictions within them. Teachers are affected by the sheer number of instant policies being published and the pressure that is then put on schools to implement them at once. There are many conflicts of interest and a great deal of power being forced on teachers from external agencies.

In the kinds of stresses that teachers talk about, in fact, the government comes out on top. Its distaste for teachers and teaching, its constant desire to manipulate, is something by which teachers themselves constantly feel burdened. Underlying this is also the sense of being got at, or 'picked on', to use the pupils' terminology, whether by managerialism or by the inquisition inflicted by Ofsted. The problem is that there is plenty of resistance to what is taking place but most of this is ineffective and ignored. There is much criticism of the politics of educational policy but this does nothing to help teachers. This is not the place to lament that fact but to address the main issues.

The main tensions

The real tensions that teachers face are deeper than those occurring presently, although we live in a time of particular discomfort. This book is about the real dilemmas of teaching which have always been on individuals' minds. All the research about teachers consistently makes some of these tensions clear.

The first tension is between the private and personal as against the public and professional. At the present time such tensions are brought to the fore since there are deliberate attacks on professionalism, and the assumption that teachers are functionaries without personal lives and instincts of their own. The fashion for such disparagement, however, is not constant and not global. The time will come when such attitudes will change. They will change as will the fashions for different types of educational research or fashions for different approaches to the teaching of reading, swinging between the emphasis on methods, and then on psychology. It is important for teachers to remember how powerful fashion is rather than being burdened by what passes away in time.

The second tension for teachers is the extent to which they are able to respond to the needs of pupils against the extent to which they are accountable to the state. Teachers always tell me that what keeps them going is the teaching itself, the pupils and their interactions. Nevertheless, teachers are seen from outside as fulfilling the requirements of statutory orders.

The greatest dilemma of all is the tension between learning and teaching. This is the heart of the teacher's problem. The teacher wants to be the person responding to individual needs, guiding and helping and fostering the natural desire to learn. Instead, a teacher is often put into the position of imposing, against other's wills, matters which seem unnatural and which will be rejected. Learning is a matter of opening up ideas; the way teaching is interpreted makes it a matter of control, an imposition that actually inhibits or destroys the desire to learn. Teachers know this well.

Other dilemmas

All dilemmas overlap but there are a number that come to teachers' minds as they discuss their work and their way of life.

The role of the teacher is a complex one. On the one hand he or she is there to deliver the curriculum. On the other hand he or she has a moral duty as a teacher who is in the position of having to keep order, demonstrate good conduct, and promote values. There are some teachers who are adamant that they are merely discharging their duties of delivery, but the expectation from parents, and the reality that all teachers understand is that they accept a responsibility for the welfare of their students and to help them learn not just facts but ideas, how to behave, values and duties. This might not be clear as a mission statement but it is the fact, even if it is inadvertent.

A teacher has a concern to help the individual learner fulfil herself. At the same time there is a pressure on the teacher to make certain that the pupil conforms, that he learns the skills that the state requires him to master. This is the kind of concern with the effects of schooling that Bowles and Gintis (1976) and King (1978), amongst many others, have highlighted. In the structure of schools there is always more than a hint of conformity, of a deliberate control, rather than the fulfilment of the individual.

Whilst the teacher is concerned with helping all individuals, there is a tension between concentrating on those who are willing and who wish to learn and excluding those who are so reluctant as to be difficult. Do teachers try to keep all reluctant pupils in the school, ignoring truancy, making certain that the school is so inclusive that all have to be there, or should the teacher accept that with the social problems that pupils bring with them, exclusion is the only answer and something that is inevitable?

Is the teacher responsible essentially to the parents of pupils as well as to the pupils themselves? Or is the teacher responsible to society as a whole, to the requirements of employment and employability, to citizenship and the responsibilities of being a useful member of society? The role of parents is an odd and complex one and, as another chapter will point out, an unused and very powerful support for teachers, but there is still a constant question of where control actually lies.

Parents are generally on teachers' sides, despite the political will to turn them into police who control what takes place in teaching. The question is whether the parents should have more real influence, as they do in a latent way in private schools. The irony about private schools, dependent on the fee-paying capacity of parents is that teachers are more respected. Teachers are also aware of the conflicting demands of the pupils and their parents, and, indeed, the influence of the local neighbourhood, and the orders of their political masters.

To what extent should teachers accept the commands and criticisms of politicians and inspectors whose influence can remain purely destructive? At what point can teachers have the confidence to ignore statutory orders?

Pupils' dilemmas

The puzzles and dilemmas of the pupils also affect teachers. One is the question of the purpose of the curriculum. Should it focus on things of interest to them or should there be a coverage of everything that needs to be known? Is there an agreement on this essential body of knowledge, or does each pupil find out what is relevant?

From the people's point of view they are 'doing a subject'. They are presented with what are often meaningless gobbets of fact and told that there are certain kinds of thought which they have got to cover. Pupils remain puzzled about the curriculum and, in the face of a lack of clarity, assume that they are there to do a core curriculum because they are told to, because it is taken to be essential, because the exams concentrate on them and because they are the underlying subjects for employment. Whilst pupils submit to this assumption they do not believe it, which creates a constant problem for them as well (Cullingford 1999).

The second dilemma for pupils is about the purpose of school. For them there is a lot of drudgery involved in school, waiting for things to happen, waiting for instructions, having to undergo a series of rote learning and meaningless tests. On the other hand, school is a place where they meet friends and can gain a great deal of satisfaction. If the purpose of schooling were made far clearer pupils would be far more content. Instead of all the factual information that is gathered together in the National Curriculum, packaged in artificial stages, there should be a reflective debate about schools. The problem is that the central issues are not addressed, partly because few dare challenge the system in case it is found wanting, and partly because it is taken for granted. The result is that teachers find themselves undermined by the pupils' lack of a sense of purpose.

Pupils wonder who is really responsible for conduct. Is the school *in loco parentis*, taking on the responsibility for order and conduct, for discipline and behaviour, or does this authority lie with the parents? Who has the moral authority to tell pupils how to behave? To what extent are teachers finding themselves, despite the lack of clarity, and despite the ambiguities of their position, especially in such a climate of fear and suspicion involving any dealings with children, having to be moral policemen?

All these questions lead to an essential dilemma of the teachers; what is their purpose? What is the real responsibility of teaching?

What is clear is that the most powerful events in school lie in the hidden curriculum, in all the latent messages and ideas that are fostered in the classroom and in the playground. Teachers need to understand that the real events in school are not the formal ones which they are controlled into carrying out, but the other ambiguous and complex arrays of relationships and understandings that are idiosyncratically derived from the experiences that are most emotional and significant, as defined by the individual pupil. In these circumstances, which is the more important: the personality of the teacher or the role he or she has to play?

Teachers need to understand what is happening in order to cope. The system is far more complicated than the simple delivery of a broad and balanced curriculum, supported by inspection and statutory orders. It would be easy for some teachers to assume that all they need to do is to fulfil orders, but all teachers, once they go beyond the simple matter of coping, have an insight into the complexities of learning that matter far more. This should not be ignored.

There is also a genuine puzzlement by teachers at the state of the education system. Is it working in the way it is supposed to? Almost every day in the main newspapers there are articles about falling standards. This is shown in terms of subjects, or sometimes in terms of overseas comparisons, sometimes in terms of the lowering of standards of examinations, sometimes in the statistics of truancy and exclusion, and sometimes in all the complaints coming from the parents or the employers and all the other onlookers who scrutinise the system. What really angers teachers is that they are the ones who are blamed for the failures of the system. No one seems to say, 'if standards are not getting better, could this be to do with policy and the way it is implemented?' Every new detailed policy, like literacy hours, seems to do more harm than good. There seems to be more unhappiness in society than ever, more divisions, more inequality, fewer skills and more complaints. These worries pass the policy makers by. Instead, they transfer blame to others as if the party system were designed just for such deflections.

Ironically, this is why teachers should not be blamed except in so far as they are the ones that keep this failing system going somehow.

The problem is that the teachers, as well as the pupils who suffer from the failings of the system and those who are responsible for the system, make it even more of the same at every sign of its failure. They merely tighten their grip.

If the dilemmas of teaching are far more complex, more pervasive and far less detailed than one might think it is because they are felt as tensions. The word 'cope' is used in this book advisedly. There are different levels of coping. It is always difficult for a teacher at first to master the basic ordering of a class of reluctant learners. There is more than a hint of the absurd in having to learn to play the role of the psychologist in keeping command of a class. The detailed psychology of divide and rule, knowing when to step in and when to step back, all these complicated forms of interaction are the first concern for the new teacher. Coping starts with being able to keep command of reluctant pupils. This is a kind of parody of government policy; the intent to force matters through control. In the teacher's case, however, this is done with great integrity and that is the difference.

After a time the concept of 'coping' takes on a somewhat different meaning. It is here that different kinds of tensions arise, when there is less distraction from day-to-day survival. The word 'cope' is used advisedly because teachers somehow have to strive in impossible circumstances. The book was going to be called *Mission Impossible* at one stage since the real problem for teachers is that they are doing something which, in the present system, is unnatural. This is made more poignant because what they love to do is the most natural thing in the world.

There is one big message: teachers are heroes but put into an impossible, even tragic position. Their missionary instincts are good. Teaching is not a selfish act but a personal one. Teachers should not be put upon in the way that they are.

From the pupils' point of view there is a fundamental flaw. They should be free of institutions, and teachers should be free to do what they do best to foster particular interests, to respond to the needs of the pupil and not the requirements of institutions. Teachers are there to help those who want to learn but who are institutionalised in a way that makes their very desire and need to learn very difficult.

This book will try to help teachers overcome some of the impossibilities and to derive real satisfaction from seeing learning take place. It is important for teachers to remember that they do much more good than they know and demonstrate, through their personalities, their unselfishness and integrity, the kind of messages that pupils need to learn.

The irony is that teachers need to support each other, to seize command of the circumstances, to work not only individually but collectively against the unnatural external controls that are put upon them.

2

The evidence

There are two major strands of evidence that belong together and which substantiate the major points of this book. The first is all the research which is to do with cognition and the functions of the brain. This neurological research has some consistent themes and agreements beneath the familiar academic arguments. The second strand of evidence comes from the pupils themselves and derive from a series of research studies that explore what and how children think, and how they analyse the experience of home and school.

Attitudes to research

It is important to remind ourselves that the research evidence over many years has been consistent, if ignored. There is a body of work that demonstrates that we know about the difference between the needs of individual children and the system that we impose on them. Much research tends to be repeated, partly because people have to learn things for themselves, as well as make their academic reputations, and partly because there is a tendency, despite the literature searches, to ignore what has been done before, especially if it is not up to the minute. The research that is referred to here, however, is more basic and unchanging, yet the findings are consistently ignored as if we did not quite dare to accept what the research tells us. Those who are offended by the conclusions of research always excuse their response by attacking the research methods. There should be no excuses for ignoring the research, especially its implications for action. This research is useful for teachers, not at the level of techniques to try out but to aid understanding of the circumstances.

If neurological research is at all instructive in its analysis of the patterns of thinking and the types of thought that are developed as a consequence, then it follows that we should take seriously what the pupils themselves say. If human beings have the capacity to criticise, analyse and understand, then all the research shows that they do so from a very young age. The problem is that although it seems fashionable to talk about listening to children, it is not really fashionable to hear what they say. We know, however, that children's views count, not only to themselves as a consequence of being listened to, but because they have a unique insight into their own states of mind and understanding. To assume that they merely regurgitate what adults say to them, or try to please by guessing what it is that they are supposed to say, is to miss the point of their understanding. It is not just an insult to young people but a disparagement of a central facet of human nature.

The question that lies like a shadow beneath the research findings is why they are not taken seriously. If we simply want an explanation for the state of the world, a response to all the worries about crime and dishonesty, an understanding about the rise of prejudice and intolerance, then we need look no further than the way in which people are brought up. Whilst we cast around for all kinds of excuses for our concerns and seek out people to blame, the facts as we know them point to the way in which people bring each other up and how their characters are formed.

The causes of suspicion

Why, then, do we not take these things seriously enough? One reason is the human fear of change. There is indifference, apathy and even a refusal to learn. We are so limited by our habits that the idea of having to rethink them is something that seems like an affront. There is much literature on change, from Machiavelli to more recent writers, and everyone knows how the most difficult thing in the world seems to be to make any fundamental change. Change is incremental and slow but it should never be a threat. What seems a threat to the people is the change in their habit of indifference. Apathy, rather than the refusal to learn, is the greatest enemy. One can find many examples of indignant and angry people who are still unwilling to participate in doing anything about it.

This is understandable as so much depends on the status quo. We have a system (of 'education') which employs a vast number of people. To suggest that it is not perfect is to make people feel an atavistic sense of threat. They have secured jobs which have personal advantages. They have families to support. There are all kinds of careers to be made in using the system as it is. People are very clever at manipulating the circumstances even if they do not believe in them. Therefore, given research findings that suggest a fundamental change, and pragmatic advice that give hints on how to earn a little bit more money, the latter will always tend to be of greater attraction.

There is very little desire to change existing systems, whether they are political or seemingly authoritative, and even if there are copious amounts of literature which shows that there are fundamental problems with them. And the world goes on much as before, despite what we know about it and however much we deplore it.

Then there is also the political desire to control. The present educational system is based on the manipulation of others, in showing prowess and the desire to make a name for a particular person, oligarchy or party. This is not the place to talk about particular political systems, but we do know that there is a tension between the central desire to control what goes on in the educational system, and the fact that the less control there is the more successful is that same system. The temptation to legislate, demonstrate action, to set targets, is too great to put aside. The system, therefore, perpetuates itself and however much it fails, the blame is always placed elsewhere. The fact that we read almost every day in almost every newspaper about the failure of tests, the lowering of standards, the lack of literacy, the bad behaviour or indifference, might lead us to think that this could be the fault of the system as it is. But this is never admitted because the desire not to change and still to control predominates.

Then there is the natural human and academic, as well as political, tradition of personal competition. Every new discovery has to be a personal one and there is no acknowledgement that others might have had the same insights. It is one of the reasons that research keeps repeating itself. The motivation is personal gain, rather than understanding. Success lies in carving out a niche for oneself, rather than sharing ideas. One of the problems for teachers is that they share rather than sell knowledge; they freely give away what they know rather than keep it to themselves by the manipulation of an arcane language of jargon.

We are up against the impediments of people not wanting to listen to evidence. Nevertheless, the evidence is emphatic and clear.

What we know about intelligence

There have been many recent advances in neurological research and all we can do here is to summarise some of the most central findings and give references to those who would be interested in taking these further. The advances in genetics have often been misinterpreted but they have reiterated some very important fundamental insights. Amongst the most central of these is that we should not any longer argue about the either/all of the nature/nurture divide since they are in such a symbiotic balance that we should, as Shakespeare did, only explore how the two factors of personality and environment interact with each other.

Recent neurological research explores in great depth the complexities of the brain. We know a great deal about the different functions of this extraordinary complicated device and the conclusions are quite clear. To some extent these are philosophical and scientific. It is fascinating for its own sake to see how the brain functions, how it interacts with the body as opposed to being a separate organ, how it has an emotional will, is full of associations and how it has such powers as well as peculiar limitations that the human condition is marked out in its understanding.

What are most important to understand are the consequences of the power of the brain. There are very major questions, like the emotional drive towards religion, and the reasons for this that people wish to find in other explanations of themselves. There are also questions about how the personality organises itself according to the culture in which it is placed. These are the familiar dilemmas in matching the human experience and the two antipodes of explaining them. What is clear is not only the power of the brain but also the fact that this power exists from a very early age. We are not dealing with limited babies but with unformed powerful minds. This has huge consequences.

We know from genetic research that at one level the variety of genes varies enormously between different animals and insects. We know that there are more genes in a firefly than in a human being. The numbers of genes are not as important as the fact that genes are learning devices (Rutter 2005). This means that the idea of a separate body and soul, like the separation of nature and nurture, is meaningless. Genes are not given characteristics of personality. Genes are responsive; a fact that makes it absolutely clear that the human mind is not just very powerful but also malleable. It has clear characteristics of its own but also adds to and amends these constantly. The acknowledgement of the power of adaptation is probably the most significant breakthrough in our understanding of human beings.

If only we took such findings seriously we could then really understand how people could be helped rather than manipulated, how we could enable the highest standards of civilisation to be manifest, rather than despair at or dismiss the possibilities of human progress. At the heart of this, of course, lies the education system.

Neurological research that demonstrates the complexity of the relationship between thinking as a rational activity and emotions, those subconscious drives that make the whole process of awareness so complex. Thinking is a far more difficult matter than to be typologised in terms of learning styles. Whilst there might be a temptation to see the difference between the 'serial' or 'holistic' learner, between the person who takes in every detail in order and skims the surface, and the person who takes in the whole and makes a structural completeness out of it, even a moment's reflection will suggest that explaining styles of thought in either of these arbitrary typologies is unhelpful. We know about the different sides of the brain. We know about Alpha waves and the way in which the whole complex mass of connections involves the distinction between one side of the cortex and the other, but to know this is not necessarily to understand the implications.

The more we know about neurology the more we know that the small psychological distinctions either of input or outcome are meaningless in themselves. There is no basis in science for learning styles, or for quite alternative approaches (say, neuro-linguistic programming) to the same subject matter beyond those obvious differences of motivation and application to which the teaching material in itself cannot be adapted.

Apart from the fact that knowing the different learning styles of students will not help the teacher, the greater problem is to do with motivation, application, the level of intensity, the desire to learn, and all the other factors that make a distinction quite simply between those who have the desire to learn and those who do not.

Thinking and society

The fact of the matter puts the responsibility on human beings to deal not only with themselves but also with the society in which they find themselves. In the research dealing with language as well as genetics (Pinker 1997) we find out about the very febrile, fragile and malleable way in which the brain operates (Rose 2005). It adapts and is resilient. It is powerful but easily influenced. There are certain conclusions to be reached from all the neurological insights that are being accumulated. There might be distinctions between one theory and another, but two facts stand out. The first is the extraordinary power of the brain from the moment it is formed. The second is its fragility, malleability and adaptability. The brain has the enormous resilience in the face of all kinds of problems, but it can also be very easily manipulated into forced obedience.

The fact that one does not know exactly at what point the brain is formed is a minor and insignificant, if interesting, problem. It has religious significance in terms of when human life comes to consciousness, but as far as teachers are concerned it is a matter of academic interest only. What matters is that the moment anybody is responding to the individual living human being he is dealing with a fully functioning, if idiosyncratic and unknowing but responsive, consciousness.

There is always a tendency in every educational system to make a distinction between those of us, as adults, who think we know everything, and those minor creatures whom we teach who are essentially ignorant and stupid, uninteresting and, as individuals, meaningless. Once a system sets up this kind of attitude it goes against all the empirical research that has taken place, and is contrary to the fundamental principles of human endeavour. That some people are wiser than others has to be accepted. But the accumulation of human wisdom needs to be passed on. What matters are not displays of brilliance but personal understanding that we have the capacity to learn from each other at any time is an essential part of the human condition but it is not always fulfilled.

The emphasis of learning is on the ability of human beings to extract information and understanding from the circumstances in which they find themselves. All kinds of inadvertent matters will be influential, not just the context like the language and beliefs, but the attitudes to other people's behaviour. The memory is idiosyncratic because it depends so much on the personal experiences and the interpretation of the personal experiences that form the mind. The mind is an instrument of enormous power and enormous vulnerability.

Emotions, language and points of view

In much of the research on young children there are certain matters that keep reappearing and remain challenging. Very young children have an enormous sympathy towards others and awareness of their points of view (Dunn 1988). The emotional understanding of each other starts in infancy when they can demonstrate levels of significant sympathy. Emotional acuteness is not just a matter of sentimentality but also a matter of intellectual insight that other people have their own status, their own dignity and their own intellectual point of view.

This implies that the ability to see that other people have different opinions, right from the start, makes the world a socially complicated place. There can be no assumptions about homogeneity of opinion, of everyone sharing a particular cultural belief as if it were an immutable fact. From the start, young children have that understanding; it is that tolerance of other people's differences that makes them unprejudiced. Prejudice and intolerance are carefully taught to them by the kind of systems in which they find themselves. The adult tendencies towards distinctions, tribalism and definitions of themselves against others, coupled with the adult attempt to create personal groups and promote their own small collective oligarchies, are what drives the young and intelligent but unformed towards the kind of sects or prejudice that so undermine human endeavour.

This means that the young understand the most crucial and complicated of all social insights. If one person has a point of view which differs from another's, this means that there is not one simple ultimate truth. Furthermore, the very young understand that people can tell lies and that a lie can be an extremely useful instrument. This insight into the way in which people operate derives from the knowledge that language is all empowering but also potentially can be used to undermine as well as create ideas. For every grand statement there can be a falsehood; language creates and can destroy. Knowing this demonstrates the most essential and sophisticated of knowledge. The problem is that our educational system is based on the assumption the young know nothing and that they have no such insights into what is really going on. Perhaps there are some who atavistically want to prevent them from developing, but we are not able to stop the young having their own insights.

Young children's understanding of philosophy, of the logic of argument, of the crucial iterative dialogue that they can have with others, is one of those instinctive attributes that should never be denied. The idea of a point of view means this point of view can be shared, can be discussed, and can be disputed. This is the excitement of learning; the realisation that a different point of view creates a theoretical framework of one's own. Language, learnt in a context of great complexity, and necessity, and at a rapid rate of even several words per day, shows the capacity and rapidity of human learning. Each word derives from an enormous background of complex meanings and ambiguities and yet a vocabulary as well as an instinctive syntactic sense is rapidly acquired. This demonstrates that the young can formulate, dispute and argue even about the very language that they use.

If language is one of those essential attributes of the human mind, so, equally instinctively, is that of numeracy. We know that the very young have to count, just to survive. As far as we can trace it back into their early gestures, the discrimination between one object and the second, between one object and the many, leads to a very basic ability in counting, an ability that, thanks to the particular ways in which we impose arithmetic upon their brains, is soon lost for the many, if still nurtured and cherished by those who have managed to understand the riches of the potential of science.

Social learning

All these matters depend on the importance of relationships. All the large research studies show it is the interaction with other people that matters. This dialogue centres on intellectual understanding. It depends sometimes on a child and sometimes on an adult, and at best both. But this intellectual relationship is not automatic and not immutable. It depends on the ability of some people to share ideas and the opportunity for that curiosity of interest in others to allow talking to take place. Children will explore their world but they know that it depends on the way in which they interact with others. Their learning is social and they need someone to share things with even when this someone can be taken over by books, a different kind of dialogue. All learning, real learning, is social, a matter of being able to explain to others what ideas are, and not simply a matter of having ideas imposed upon them (Wells 1985, Richman et al. 1982).

The creative part of the mind, the spontaneous ability to see things in their own way is also often reiterated thanks to the refutation of the Piagetian ideas of a kind of mental inevitability of the different stages in the presentation of ideas. Donaldson (1993) and other researchers have demonstrated that the ability to understand any ideas depends upon the cultural context in which they are presented. The desire to prove different stages of ability, like different stages of moral reasoning, might be an interesting academic game but it has distracted people from the essentials of learning and the consequences.

Reasoning, logic and scientific understanding all depend on exploration. There is no point in telling children the rules of physics in an abstract way when they so clearly discover these things by experiment. All studies of teaching practice (Harlen 1985) show the natural curiosity about the world that needs to be nurtured by a sharing of personal explorations of ideas. Science is exciting when there is a reason for it. The imposition of stale facts and theories is nothing compared to the physical and intellectual exploration of the universe. Understanding the way that the mind develops should lead to an awareness of what to do about it.

All this depends on the difference between the facts that are imposed on pupils and their desire to explore and question the meaning of such facts. All the rote learning that is believed in so intensely, all the skills that are supposed to be instrumental become of no value compared to the motivation and desire to learn. This is not a matter of 'creativity', sometimes a meaningless term, but a matter of trying to engage the young mind with the reality of the environment.

The capacity of pupils

All the research that is invoked here is about neurology, and about the capacity of young children to think for themselves. The other important body of research comes from the children themselves and from the outcomes of what they say. Children give evidence by questioning and exploring, not dismissing ideas in a prejudiced way but the wanting to get to the bottom of them. They're all like St Thomas, doubting and having to explore empirically. They are also like Voltaire, suspicious and wanting to know the truth. Children are analytical, critical, sympathetic, understanding, and usually silent about their ideas.

The research which is the basis for the conclusions of this book is based on many years of interviews with young children, on hundreds and hundreds of transcripts and on many publications, a few which will be summarised here.

There was a time when the tradition of research depended purely on the instrumental. Large-scale studies including control groups and comparisons based on experimental models dominated. The idea of finding out what was going on inside people's minds, and how they could react, let alone the very idea of studying cognition, was unusual.

When I began researching children's response to television, I was considered extremely eccentric for not relying on experimental models. The research at the time could be typified by the studies in which children would be led into a classroom to watch a video and then be led into another room where the same objects might be placed to see if they imitated the actions they had seen on the screen. I tried to find out, instead, what they had actually watched and tried to explore the truth of what they had seen as opposed to their attempt to please the interviewer. I also made no assumptions based on large hypotheses about copying or imitating. This research revealed that children would talk clearly and openly not only about what they had seen but what they prefer, not only about the programmes that interested them, but their styles of viewing and how it fitted in to the rest of their lives. This wealth of data unearthed broader questions about the experience that children have.

If children were able to talk about their experience of watching television in such analytical detail it follows that they should be able to reveal the actual experience they had of school (Cullingford 1991). In place of the many assumptions that we have about what takes place in school, the curriculum, the ordering about of people, the rules and regulations, children, especially in primary school, revealed their own experience of what is was actually like and what mattered to them. This opened up the whole question of the hidden curriculum and all the other events that were of such importance to the pupils. They talked about teachers and they talked about subjects but they also talked about each other, the playground and the way in which they learned what was important to them. They revealed that they understood the latent messages as clearly as the artifice by which the curriculum was manipulated.

The research then went on to explore the experience of school as a community but in larger terms. The same concern to discover attitudes, sources of information and ways of thinking were pursued in children's views of society as a whole. They talked about their attitude to politics and to the police; they talked about their attitudes to crime and punishment. They revealed how diminished they felt and ignored by the higher echelons of power. They had a clear sense of societies and unfairness, not only in this country but also of the contrasts between countries, with huge gaps between the rich and the poor and between the powerful and the ignored. A whole clear understanding of society was revealed, often despite what they had been told in school, since citizenship was not even notionally on the agenda (Cullingford 1992).

The research went on to explore the deeper levels of human experience, looking at the ways in which the experience of home related to that of school. Their sense of the world as a whole, their neighbourhoods, their friends, and the symbols of success and failure as seen in the media, all blended into an acute sense of themselves in relation to others. The assumption that young children had no sense of perspective, nor a clear point of view, was overwhelmed by the evidence that shows their attitudes towards themselves in relation to others at a variety of levels, and demonstrates how they formed their own attitudes towards the psychological motivations for behaviour. Many of the experiences that they revealed were far bleaker than had been anticipated; not deliberate distortions of normal life, but as a part of a normal fabric of everyday experience. What they revealed about school made one question even more vital: whether this was a rite of passage that does more harm than good.

The next major piece of research explored the experience of those who had become excluded from society and had ended up in prison. These young people, once knowing that none of what they would say would be revealed to the authorities, talked, as all people do, openly and relieved that they have someone with whom to talk. What was of concern was not what they had done wrong so that they had become criminals but the experiences that led to them behaving as they did, and when the influences first became apparent. There are a number of layers explored in *The Causes of Exclusion* (Cullingford 1999) and these all demonstrated how there were certain factors that were extremely important to all of them, starting from the attitudes of their parents, through peer group influences to the experience of school and the almost inevitable exclusion. The final and almost invariably explosive leaving of school, following on from series of truancies of one kind or another and the influence of peer groups was merely the ultimate point of a long and consistent experience which entailed being ignored. Many of the every day experiences of pupils were here, but in extreme forms.

In the typologies of parenting there are extremes of authoritarian control and *laissez-faire*. All these young people found themselves with parents who for one reason or another were indifferent to them. At first these young people felt this was a great thing; they could do what they wanted. Looking back, however, they realised that this was disastrous for them. It threw them into the hands of others of equal self-indulgence in neighbourhoods where are all kinds of nefarious activities were encouraged. The tragedy of the analysis that these young people gave was that they felt that they would be the same as their own parents and cause the same effect; because of their temperament and their tendency to be easily provoked they felt likely to find themselves in trouble yet again. The sense of realism, the fragility of their experiences, and their potential to be prevented, were all very clear.

Peer pressure, becoming part of a gang, or becoming part of a small group defined against the rest of society, whether in school or outside, was very important to these young people (Harris 1998). This led to an exploration of why people become prejudiced against each other. Again, given anonymity and confidentiality, young people talk clearly about their sense of tribalism, of being part of a small secure group. Groups define themselves against others and create out of a kind of shared experience a simple and primitive psychological feeling of shared identity. This was, once again, a demonstration of how young people think, feel and react. Their lack of strong personality in the sense of being able to make their own moral decisions, because of their upbringing, led them to be both malleable to other's ideas and resentful of them. The school was seen to be an important part in promoting prejudice for all kinds of reasons. The kind of information that the children acquired, and the insights they had into both official and unofficial behaviour, led them to a hardening of their own position and a suspicion of others.

If *The Inner World of the School* (Cullingford 1991) mostly explored children in their last year of primary school and the first year of secondary school, *The Best Years of Their Lives? Pupils' Experiences of School* (Cullingford 2002), looked at pupils in years 10 and 11 who reflected on their experience. Again, they questioned the core curriculum and its lack of a clear sense of purpose. They felt the school had never had a clear purpose beyond the obvious one of being a rite of passage to become employed and they regretted not only their own failures but the fact that they could never get to know teachers properly. Major themes of this book also included that there is a real need for human relationships with others as opposed to playing the roles of control and obedience. *The Best Years of Their Lives?* turned out to be an ironic title since most of the basis of educational policy, from competition and tests to targets and skills, was disparaged and dismissed by the pupils. What pupils in the end realised they had learned most from school was how to deal with other people, whether those in authority or their peers.

Young people are clearly intelligent, and they are vulnerable to all kinds of influence. They need intellectual relationships with other people and are also exposed to a huge amount of information which they have analysed for themselves. In *How Pupils Cope with School* (Cullingford 2008) their attitudes towards all the influences on their lives were made clear, from home to neighbourhood and from school to the larger society. Again, it was clear that what they were presented with was not what they would most like in an ideal world. But it was equally clear that they felt that they had to submit to it. The fact that they resented doing so was even clearer. Nevertheless, with resilience and with that human capacity to survive difficult events, they showed they had come through.

These are brief glimpses of research studies all substantiating a great deal of evidence, added to by innumerable doctorate theses by research students exploring the inner lives of children. The evidence abounds. I choose to draw attention to one particular body of it, but this cannot be, in terms of evidence, unique, even if its interpretation is. Young people have clear views about their lives and are very articulate about it. We disbelieve them at our peril. It is an insult to young people to assume that they are not clear about what is happening. It is also a dismissal of all the neurological research which makes it clear that young people are articulate, analytical, logical and precise in their judgements.

The whole evidence suggests something that is essentially pragmatic. Those who worry about society need to look at what we are doing to bring up new generations. Those who feel uncomfortable at the way that teachers have to perform in the present climate need to be aware that the pupils understand the difficulties and are sympathetic with them, but would like, as teachers would, something quite different.

Conclusions

We can summarise the basic findings of the research:

1. The brain power of young children is formidable, even if it appears idiosyncratic, and unshaped by adults.
2. Intellectual relationships are crucial from the start.
3. There is no simple divide between body and mind (or soul).
4. Neither nurture nor nature ever dominates; although we can do something about the former.
5. Young people are analytical and articulate, given the chance.
6. What young people need and what they are given are not the same.

3

Policies within and outside school

In the outline of research it was reported how consistent the findings are at a fundamental level. The particular examples here and the voices of pupils and teachers come from a case study that involved six secondary schools offered extra money to try out an alternative approach to the standard curriculum; at least for some. What it revealed is that even at an official level some to the dilemmas are at least recognised up to a point, even if they are so much better understood by teachers.

This book is about tensions, essentially between the needs of learners and what is provided for them, and the difficulties of those caught in the middle – the teachers. The teachers themselves are not part of the provision; they are the ones who are supposed to 'deliver' it. Teachers are part of the learning process, and that distinguishes them from the managerial process.

The position of teachers

Many of the underlying conflicts in the education system are not hidden; the disappointment with standards of literacy and numeracy, let alone social behaviour, remain. They are even officially acknowledged. The newspapers carry reports about the disquiet of universities and employers about the products of the system, and the many different political initiatives suggest that some of the flaws in the system are obvious even if denied.

Teachers are sensitive to the comments and the disquiet, but it can be to our advantage to question and follow a different path. One of the concerns most often publicly aired is between the Standard Assessment Tests, the imposition of targets and the question of whether these are really effective or even relevant. Many people question whether what is offered to all the pupils is appropriate.

As a result of this concern and because of the lack of clarity or a clear sense of vision and purpose, teachers are caught between questions of the academic and the vocational and there are many small experiments in tinkering with the National Curriculum as a result. Is the driving force of education higher standards in personal achievement or in those skills useful for employment?

The fact that the purpose of the curriculum is not clear allows teachers to ask more fundamental questions, and one means of survival is to know about the evidence that acknowledges there might be problems. In a centrally controlled system any alternative thinking tends to be not just dismissed but ridiculed. There is, in the culture of blame and mistrust, a strong element of arrogance and disparagement. Teachers do not deserve to be the target of such attitudes; it is clear that the very system has its grave limitations.

Teachers therefore need evidence to support their cause. Every week there are signs of acknowledgment that things might not be perfect and these need to be seized. There are many questions about relevance and whilst these tend to be limited to the vocational elements, they raise more fundamental questions. What follows in this chapter is a case study of a typical initiative that reveals the flaws of the system and the way that the pupils and teachers adjust to an alternative approach. It demonstrates the way in which in the everyday life of the school – full of the signs of the struggle to cope, survive and to keep going – there are the symptoms of a deeper tension, brought to the surface by an additional temporary scheme with extra resources and when the resources are used up, confined to oblivion.

Teachers are caught between the interests of pupils and the concerns of policy makers. They feel this daily and have to resolve the tensions, so that the more they understand about the ambiguities the better they can deal with them. Schools are like microcosms of society and mimic the tensions between the individual and society, the conflict between rights and responsibilities, and between personal needs and institutional demands. This is the theoretical framework of sociology ('structure' and 'agency') but it is a real and practical problem.

The art of teaching is an individual activity, even if learning is social. Both learning and teaching are intuitive, emotional and expressive and both contrast with the demands of schooling as a system. The factors that make life difficult for pupils and teachers are nearly all to do with the implacable system, and this is what both complain about. The problem is that the system attempts to impose itself with as little flexibility as it can get away with.

Policies and reality in education

Official policy is based on an assumption that schools are complete in themselves, in entire command of their own destinies and therefore accountable for all that takes place. Schools are seen as hermeneutic, as if they were cut off from socio-economic forces and unaffected by the backgrounds and circumstances of their pupils. Whilst a glance at the league tables makes clear the link between success and social advantage, the enactment of policy ignores this basic fact. The success of schools seems measured by academic outcomes and not by social difficulties, and many teachers find themselves in a contradictory position of battling with social forces that are not taken into account.

The formal curriculum itself embodies this contradiction. The statutory orders are firm and clear. Within the framework of a 'broad and balanced' curriculum, the material that is supposed to be given to the pupils is not only detailed and comprehensive but even supported by directions about how it should be taught. The central subjects of the core curriculum, particularly English and mathematics, dominate and the testing system underlines the importance of knowledge and information. The 'non-statutory' requirements of the National Curriculum, however, stress more value-based issues. The contrast between what is essential and what is desirable is clear. For the majority of teachers and perhaps all pupils, this is not immediately apparent since they feel the weight of the central curriculum in a way that suggests a unifying purpose and power, to which all other issues are marginal (Elliott 1998, Cullingford 2002). Even if other issues are recognised as existing, they are not considered useful enough to be measured in the same way.

The differences between schools are clear, but they are also repeated within schools. There are contrasts in alternative attitudes to learning and in the ways that pupils view the relevance or irrelevance of the curriculum. Inequalities abound, not just in the outcomes but in the attitudes of pupils and their understanding of the academic demands. In almost every school there are those who lack academic self-belief. The disjunction between the language that is used at some homes and the language used at school has long been recognised (Heath 1983). Those pupils who have had a long experience of intellectual dialogue, sharing ideas and definitions, will always find school far easier to cope with than those who are accustomed to using language in a far less discriminating way. It is not the amount of language used at home that counts but the way that language is used. Those pupils to whom iterative dialogue is alien spend their intellectual energies in trying to guess what the teacher wants them to say. For some pupils the difficulties in conforming to the demands of the formal curriculum are never overcome, and some suggest that the education system fosters inequalities through competition and certain types of cognition.

The league tables and the examination results demonstrate the significant differences between schools, a difference that is generally agreed to be growing. This distinction between schools is not, however, just a simple matter of the differences of intake, or the result of parental choice by that minority of parents who possess a choice. These might perpetuate the difference, but within schools there takes place an internalisation of certain social attitudes, a reflection on, and deepening of, the attitudes outside. In what can be termed 'psychological exclusion' pupils not only remain quiet and invisible in the routines of school but have their sense of inferiority reinforced (Cullingford 1999). They see perpetuated the significance of their subordinate position compared to others. Pupils are, after all, fully aware of the reputation of schools they attend and their place in the hierarchies of society. In every school, the awareness of external control, as in the imposition of testing, affects every pupil and every teacher from the beginning.

Those pupils who are in under-resourced inner city schools are denied the kinds of choices that middle-class parents so determinedly pursue. They are aware of a sense of social exclusion both within the school and in its circumstances. All the socio-economic factors that surround schools are also perpetuated within them, underlining sets of shared values and habits. Schools exemplify the tensions between their own presumed hegemony and all the external forces that they are surrounded by – the soft social forces of parents, pupils and teachers, each with their own values, the contradictions of private feeling and thwarted ambition, and the hard forces of political expectation, results and inspection.

Policies, reality and pupils

The pupils experience the tensions between the complexities of learning, containing many different practices, beliefs and needs, and the seemingly simple delivery of the curriculum. Knowledge is presented as if it were a model of efficiency and effectiveness, as if by its very delivery the pupils' needs were met. For many pupils this emphasis on statutory delivery means that their own needs appear to be rebuffed. They cannot participate in the ways they long for, but are expected to acquire the knowledge delivered to them.

The ways in which the pupils understand what is presented to them depends on their understanding of the purpose behind the curriculum, whether they are engaged in it or simply submitting to what is given to them. What is relevant to pupils is not necessarily the same as what is presented to them.

The tensions within many schools, especially those with difficult catchment areas, arise from the different types of personal engagement which compete with each other, like the difference between the statutory and the non-statutory orders, like the contrasts between the apparent choices led by market forces and the way that choice is commandeered by a minority. Whilst there appears to be an estrangement in many young people from the official political will, and suspicion of political motivation and debate, this does not mean that young people are socially unengaged, let alone socially unaware. Whilst the public edifice of the education system might be associated with the politics of party domination, the realities of the everyday, within and outside school, continue. Pupils might not trust politicians and their policies but they have to live with them.

The problem for many pupils is that this juxtaposition between external will and personal liability confronts them all the time. Within the cultures of schools there are very different notions of who is included and how inclusion is viewed. On the one hand we meet the assumption that teachers, teaching assistants and children are passive recipients of an outsiders' curriculum. On the other hand we should also be aware of the unspoken but deeply felt observations of the individual children, those who would articulate their own perception of the conflicting pedagogies of fact and values, if only they had a chance to do so.

Tensions in schools

Whatever the circumstances of individual schools and their place in the socio-economic diaspora of market forces and manipulated choice, and whatever the contradiction of external and internal forces, schools are complex places that reflect the conflicts that surround them. The evaluative judgements from outside – what is a 'good school' or an 'effective school' – do not do justice to what goes on within. If we look at schools as real communities we need to listen to the experience of the participants. Each of these, pupils and teachers, seek their own agendas and try to balance the often conflicting demands.

Schools themselves embody the contradictions of demands. Pupils and teachers are aware of the complexities of balancing official policy and social reality. To what extent do they feel that the curriculum is a burden rather than an entitlement? To what extent do they wish to pursue something quite different, perhaps related directly to the outside world, like work placements and work experience? To what extent would schools wish to make greater differentiations between pupils and their curriculum? Would parents prefer an alternative? And are the central skills associated with the core curriculum really more important than the social skills of collaboration and understanding? Schools are aware of the tensions, the conflicts between the autonomy of tests and their relevance to the home, and the social and economic environment.

Teachers, if not policy makers, are aware of the differences between the learning that takes place within the classroom and outside. There are many sources of information that lie beyond the scope of the school. There are many types of information available through computers. Teachers not only know the different demands and expectations of their pupils but rate out-of-class learning surprisingly highly, appreciating the social aspects of learning as well as the need of individuals. And yet, teachers feel constrained by the demands of objective measurement.

The National Curriculum, with its attendant regime of testing and inspection has been in place in the United Kingdom for more than twenty years, influencing a whole generation; in essentials it has not changed during that time. The central idea remains, based on a core curriculum and a standardised content – not chosen by the teacher – together with key stages and tests. Whilst the major critics of the whole enterprise have been ignored, there have been many minor adjustments to subjects or to themes like personal and social education and citizenship. The debates about the curriculum have been essentially marginalised to small choices or adaptations, like the introduction of more information and communication technology (ICT) and the strengthening of the core, or the allowance for sport or other activities. The statutory orders remain in place. At the same time schools collectively and teachers individually have found themselves adept at pursuing their own concerns, and at interpreting the curriculum in their own way.

The way that teachers adapt the curriculum to their own needs has two levels. The usual one is the unofficial freedom of manoeuvrability and interpretation. But there are occasional opportunities that are officially sanctioned. There are rare 'disapplication' orders that, in their wording, show how powerful the National Curriculum orders are and how exceptional any official endorsement of change is. These minor official adjustments suggest a reluctant realisation that some of the more marginalised pupils – those unwilling or unable to keep up – should have some allowances made for them.

An example of pupils' and teachers' attitudes to the curriculum

There are occasional initiatives to allow certain schools to introduce an experimental programme to let selected pupils to be withdrawn from mainstream lessons and participate in alternative activities, from sport to work experience. When this takes place it throws into question the attitudes of teachers and pupils, in their last official year of schooling, to the existing curriculum, to subjects like foreign languages, design technology and science from which they could be released, and to the benefits of an alternative curriculum as they near the end of compulsory schooling.

Any alternative to the standard model that is made available to schools is seized upon. This is partly because if any school or any authority hears of any extra resources that are available they will gladly take the opportunity and will apply for extra support before they even know what it is for. This is itself a telling comment on schools. But any help in lending support for alternative approaches to the curriculum is always welcome, since schools are often trying to find other, unofficial means of keeping the system going.

Schools are always trying to accommodate the more difficult pupils as well as protecting those who do not want to be distracted by them. Alternative provision, in contrast to the formal curriculum, is seen as good for motivation but also like a reward for disaffection. There is inevitably an equivocal attitude amongst teachers and pupils to those who are not part of the mainstream, as if they are deemed to have failed in some way. Indeed, alternative programmes tend to be associated with the disaffected, not as recognition of a genuinely interesting alternative but as a grudging recognition that something has to be done. Any alternative to the standard curriculum tends to be for a minority, who themselves are assumed to be deficient in some way.

Alternatives to the standard provision of schools, the central curriculum and its testing, are often looked at askance, as if they were a sign of failure, of a submission to those who refuse to conform. But pupils and teachers know that there are other ways of being educated so any chance to try them out is relished. When pupils compare the standard fare with other opportunities they are clear what seems to them more worth while, but most pupils still associate such education with a failure to conform and their jealousy is mitigated by the relief of not being labelled or associated with a lack of proper submission and concentration.

The pupils who need alternative provision demonstrate some of the peculiar tensions amongst groups in school. They are both self-selected and picked out by teachers but this distinction is quickly meaningless since they were almost the same. All seem to know who the disaffected are, however quiet they might be. The teachers' judgements coincide with the pupils' own judgements as well as those of their peers. All agree about who are the ones most 'disaffected', 'difficult' or 'slow'. The pupils label themselves as if there were implicit understandings amongst all involved. More pupils want to be 'disapplied' from the National Curriculum than can be. Teachers have to restrict the numbers since a chance to escape from the routine is so popular. There is an interesting ambiguity about whether the other pupils, pursuing their own goals as usual, are jealous of, or despise, the special groups which are withdrawn from normal lessons. On the whole they look on them with mixed feelings, wishing they could do likewise, but relieved that such a wish would not disturb their concentration on the task in hand.

Pupils' comments on the standard curriculum and the alternative: a case study

Nothing reveals pupils' attitudes to the curriculum and their general experience of school more clearly than their reactions to being allowed to escape from it. Even if the kinds of experiences that are offered were not as exciting as they would have wished, any experience is considered preferable to what had gone before. They feel that any escape from the routines of normal schooling is a sign of freedom from a meaningless constraint and of more relevance. They share a strong sense that the school experience as presented to them has no real purpose. The implacable curriculum is seen as a given but it is not really believed. They do not recall anyone saying what the purpose is. All the subjects, all the tests and even the styles of delivery, take on the guise of a mechanical routine.

The everyday experience of school is seen as relentless and unrewarding. They guess that the underlying if unspoken purpose is to prepare them for employment. This makes them question whether all the subjects they took have any direct relevance to jobs. The irony is that by not spelling out the purposes of the curriculum – the overall phrase 'broad and balanced' conveys very little to pupils – some of the prevailing assumptions, as detected by pupils, are that the central skills are paramount. They have been told they need skills and they assume that these skills of literacy, numeracy and ICT are to prepare them for employment. Any other sense of purpose in school, like pleasure, excitement, the pursuit of truth, moral awareness or creativity, does not cross their minds in the same way. This is a reflection on what the pupils constantly imbibe from the messages officially conveyed to them. The word they use most to justify their attendance at school is that it is 'necessary' but they do not say for what. Those who say they find school 'useful' cannot say why. They all realise that the everyday experience of school is a tension between submission and rebellion, between fulfilling expectations or failing to do what is asked. They know they are expected to do 'good work', and define this clearly as being what pleases or satisfies the teachers. On the other hand most associate school as a place for 'getting into trouble'. When they are asked to say how this happened the telling phrase 'for answering back' is invariably used. This implies a challenge, a questioning, a threat to the prevailing ethos of unswerving acceptance and submission.

The alternative programmes to the standard curriculum that young people are offered are often part of the school programme. They are run by familiar teachers. Yet any different programme is seen as something quite separate, quite distinct from the normal routines of school. The pupils all define them as 'getting away from school'. What they mean is not a physical distance but a mental stance. By being differentiated, for whatever reason, they feel more individual. By being removed from the large class, they feel, for good or bad, singled out. Whilst they realise that this is more likely for nefarious reasons than good ones, they nevertheless feel that they are, by this demonstration of difference, valued for the first time. This suggests something about the psychology of the 'gang', of those who do not fit. They know there are pockets of discontent, but they also associate this with independence and questioning, a well as disaffection or anti-social behaviour. The independence of rebellion is a demand for some notice.

Special programmes give pupils a sense of individuality. This is partly because they are doing things by themselves, like tutoring others or working in a factory. It was also partly because they no longer feel part of an anonymous mass of people all doing the same thing. What they most value, and which gives them their sense of distinction, is their changed relationship with teachers. They are able to have real conversations, one to one, with adults. They are adamant that this was not normally possible:

Normal teachers don't have the time. (boy, age 14)

Instead of feeling themselves to be a nuisance in 'normal' classes, where any individual attention could be a distraction, they feel that their relationship with teachers as individuals was a real possibility. It gives them self-esteem. They find they can have open-ended conversations. They realise that not all contributions they made had to be a response to closed questions. There is no longer the sense of a one-way system of conversation as a form of testing. The lack of the normal tensions with teachers, and indeed with their peer group, makes them feel more confident:

It makes us feel good in yourself. (girl, age 14)

This points to the fact that in the normal routines of classrooms they feel they did not count. Any individual attention is interpreted as negative. Every time they drew attention to themselves in normal classes they were seen as trouble, as going against the collective endeavour of the curriculum.

One of the outcomes of alternative programmes is a renewed questioning of the experience they had been undergoing for so many years. They begin to wonder what the purpose was:

Why can't they say what it is for? i.e. for your education? (girl, age 14)

They feel that they had been under pressure for years without really understanding why. They had been cajoled into working at tasks, which was alright 'as long as you do your best', 'but we had never been told why they were doing them'. These are the phrases that keep being repeated. Such a fundamental analysis of the prevailing ethos of schools is plainly and often expressed by pupils when they are given the chance to do so. There is usually no expectation that pupils might reflect on their experience. There is, perhaps, a fundamental fear that such questioning is dangerous. Given the chance, pupils not only articulate the differences between their present and previous experiences but feel they are – for the first time in years – being treated as individuals with potential rather than as pupils failing to meet targets. They are taken away from a deep sense of failure or potential failure. Their relationships with teachers can become the start of a sense of confidence.

The removal of some pupils from the normal cohort caused mixed reactions amongst the majority left behind who felt both envy and relief. The pupils who had been taken out of the class to be placed in the programme felt no stigma for being separated from the usual lessons. They did not think that their 'mates were jealous'. On the contrary, they suggested that:

Being a drop-out is good for the rest, for the good ones. (boy, age 13)

Whilst their own self-esteem had risen they still recognised themselves to be amongst the failing ones. Without them there to hold the rest back, the class could get on. They had no problem with this. The psychological discrimination between the successful and unsuccessful had always been embedded in the system of classes and classrooms; all that had now happened was that it was officially recognised.

The pupils who were deemed to be the more successful ones, who fitted in, also expressed some relief to have certain pupils taken away:

It's so much better without Joe; we can get on now. (girl, age 13)

One of the uses of an alternative programme is the removal of 'trouble-makers', those who cause disruption by too much talk or the inability to concentrate. Outside the classroom they are no longer a trouble. The sense of rebellion, or antipathy to the routines of school, is not to do with any fundamental antipathy to society or teachers or work or even the social world that is a fundamental part of the school. It is the demands of the standard curriculum – the official routines. Whilst some of the pupils felt relief at the removal of the 'disapplied', others did feel a pang, despite the feeling that they could get on undisturbed:

Why can't I have access to the resources like IT and key skills? (boy, age 14)

The mainstream pupils are intrigued by the idea of going outside school and gaining work experience. On the whole, however, the separation of classes into those who could manage the normal routines and those who found it more difficult was a mutual relief. It was one of the minorities who were following the alternative route who remarked:

There are too many time wasters here. They leg it. I can't keep up with the work (boy, age 14)

Teachers' reactions to the curriculum and its alternative

The prevailing attitudes of teachers can be summarised succinctly: they all express a profound sense of relief that an opportunity had been given them to offer an alternative programme of work. They not only felt that such an alternative to the normal routines of school was necessary but they would have liked to have been able to extend it to many other pupils; indeed, some suggested it should be available to all. The only drawback they saw was the limited funding, in terms of numbers of pupils and length of time. The teachers wondered why there should be such a sudden and short-term opportunity. They felt that it should have been built into the mainstream of schooling much earlier.

Naturally, some of the reasons for welcoming the opportunity were pragmatic reactions to difficult pupils. Both the disaffected and the less able (referred to as 'weak but willing') were accommodated and the mainstream could get on without such impediments, thereby giving the school a better chance to raise its exam scores. The programme was a way of dealing with the disaffected, but the teachers had more important things to say. They felt that such an opportunity was not only needed because they were struggling with some pupils but because they were struggling with the curriculum. By this stage they, as well as pupils, were very tired of it:

The National Curriculum has too many restraints.

They felt that it did not allow 'an individual approach to learning'. The more flexible programme offered individual relationships. The teachers understood this. Whether they were offering pleasurable things like a sport of an amusement, or helping in work experience, the teachers realised that they were able to concentrate on social and emotional skills, on confidence and self-sufficiency, on a sense of purpose and the chances of fulfilment:

For some this is a new start.

They see a goal, a reason for doing it, a prospect of a job.

They would have dropped by the wayside.

Whilst the teachers realised that they were dealing with problem pupils, they felt that the problem went deeper than the minority being helped and that the problem did not lie simply in the pupils. The sense of exclusion was part of the system rather than the pathology of the individuals. When the teachers pointed out the usefulness of the programme it was because they shared the pupils' sense that it was 'relevant'. They kept repeating this:

They know they are doing something relevant.

This says something about the curriculum as it stands. For many teachers and pupils the National Curriculum is not relevant.

Teachers, like their pupils, are involved in survival techniques that allow little time for reflection. There are targets to be met and subjects to be covered. They are responding to new initiatives whilst dealing with fundamental social problems. They are often distracted from the 'non-statutory' tasks by statutory duties. They are trying to do their best for their pupils, at the same time they feel undermined by the realisation that there are larger external forces that they cannot control. There is no differentiation in the curriculum. The very 'entitlement' is a burden for a significant number of pupils.

Teachers realise that they can do little about many of the problems their pupils face. They are constrained by the system and yet long to make a difference to their pupils. It is as if the teachers themselves exemplified the tensions between the external and internal forces. The very welcome that the teachers gave to an opportunity to meet the pupils' needs by being less constrained reveals a great deal. The teachers felt that they were in a system that through the doctrine of parental choice gave them great problems. Certain schools were left with skewed intakes; once a school has a weakening reputation it is difficult to avoid being a sink school, with parents shunning it whenever possible:

We have to take bad kids, the GCSEs will be poor, and we will be in trouble.

'Bad kids' are more usually referred as 'difficult pupils'. The irony is that despite the downward spiral the teachers do not admit to the problems being intractable. They still tried 'on the pastoral side' by compensating where they could. The 'bad kids' were not being labelled but assessed realistically and laconically. The teachers use phrases like 'the dehumanisation of schools' and of the 'fundamentally weird world of school survival'.

The contrast between the every day routines of school and the potential for something different are very clear. The teachers knew that for many pupils the National Curriculum was a burden:

Fifty per cent of them think lessons are irrelevant; many don't come to school.

Against this, alternative programmes are a godsend, a merciful relief. The teachers saw it as 'a new start.

Conclusions

The evidence presented by this case study demonstrates vehement, shared feelings. The schools might think of themselves as 'sink' schools but they are typical of any other inner city schools nationwide. The sense of helplessness, even despondency, is widespread. It does not mean that the teachers do not care; on the contrary, their frustration is evidence that they wish things could be different, and that they will meanwhile try to mitigate the circumstances as best they can.

The levels of stress in teachers, as well as the well documented turnover, is established as is the development of a new generation of teachers who are learning to see themselves in a different way, with a type of mechanical professionalism. Here we see stress rather than adaptation, and this includes the advisors and the head teachers, as well. It is as if pupils and teachers shared constant frustration.

The evidence that is accumulated here is easy to summarise, and has a consistency that does not need artificial 'problematising'. There are few variables to play with; rather a clear picture of the deeply held feelings that are rarely given a voice. The vehemence of the feelings ran throughout the conversations, formal and informal, with the teachers and pupils alike. Their very relief at being released from the every day demands revealed unexpected depths of usually unarticulated concern. The clash of the rigidity of the National Curriculum and the effects of parental choice led to a sense of being beleaguered and helpless in the face of outside forces. The way that the schools leaped at the chance to do something different, to deal with a long-standing problem was itself revealing. The faintest chance of some extra funding excited the teachers even before they realised what it was for. When they understood the purpose the great question was 'why this should be short term?' Why release pupils from drudgery and teachers from the impossible demands of control, only to plunge them back after a while?

Schools are meshed between complex internal and external forces. They are aware of the context in which they operate and the strength of external decisions. This is reflected in the tensions within schools. Who are really the 'included' and who the excluded when pupils were given a choice of their own? In one way the mainstream remained the favoured group, the one approved of by the system; they could get on with the demands without so much disruption. In another way the pupils also felt that the minority of pupils on the programme were favoured; their questioning of the relevance of the curriculum had been rewarded. It was they who were seen to benefit from something relevant and worthwhile. Here, inclusion and exclusion saw a reversal of roles.

4

The pupils' experience of school

What pupils acknowledge

The moment children enter school they become different from before. They have had to add a new dimension to their lives, one that they take very seriously. In school they are part of a large group, one amongst many. They are no longer simply individuals. They have to submit to rules and learn a new type of language. They have to learn to adapt to controls and to show constraint.

Schools also offer contact with many other people, with new excitements and new activities. Some children find that the pleasures are many and adapt to the restraints with ease. Others find the new challenges permanently difficult, and that they are unprepared for demands. The ability to submit to the demands of school depends on the resilience learned in the early years, on the parents and their attitudes, on the language and relationships employed at home, and on the subsequent confidence and motivation that they bring. About such atavistic attitudes schools can do little.

It is, however, important to remember that school is a distinct and significant experience for all children, and one that needs to be understood. It is very easy for us, as teachers, given the implacability of the system, to forget what it is like to be a pupil. With all the crowding of the curriculum, the policies and the policing of policies, the sheer number of pupils and the heavy demands on time, it is natural to think of pupils as a mass, as groups to be controlled and organised. There is little time to think of them as individuals, except those who stand out.

It is as individuals that pupils think of themselves, even as they adapt to the demands of playing a role. In the typologies of the way that pupils adapt, there are normally three groups which are described. One group are those who draw attention to themselves in a positive way, who like to joke and cajole, who know how far to go with humour, without causing disruption. Another group are those who are psychologically disaffected and who cling to each other in subversive groups for support, resenting the fact that they are made to play a role. All routines are taken personally, and the sense of being forced to do things prevails. The third group is the vast majority who quietly submit and who strive to remain invisible (Pye 1989). When we think back on classes we taught years ago we will always remember only a few of the children. These will include the most difficult as well as the most interesting. The majority will have faded from our minds.

Whatever the way in which children react to the demands of school, they all share the same insights into what is taking place. They see the hierarchies of control, both in the formal settings and in the private hidden spaces of the school experience. They see the significance of power and the demands of their submission. The school is a microcosm of society and what is learned about societies, communities and politics is shaped by the experiences of school.

It is hard for teachers, given the burdens they have to bear and the demands of control, to see the point of view of pupils. It is hard enough to find time to see them as individuals, but teachers do their best to overcome all impediments. It is harder still to see the inner life of the idiosyncratic hidden views that all individuals in the class bring with them. Their private lives, their sense of the meaning of life and their personal beliefs are not supposed to have anything to do with the curriculum. It is simply a different world from the targets, the tasks and the tests that dominate school life.

One reason that the private thoughts and ideas of pupils remain unknown is the fact that they are supposed to be kept apart from the formalities of the curriculum. They are not meant to be recognised. Whilst there are nevertheless many attempts to do otherwise, involving parents, involving psychiatrists, including pupils in decision-making, every teacher will know that these activities, however laudable, are not essential to the National Curriculum and its delivery. At the core, the individual lives of pupils are not the point of subject knowledge and success in examinations.

Another reason for the hidden lives of individuals lies in the fact that pupils themselves are reticent. They do not wish to bring their home lives into the strictures, the tenets and the ethos of school. They recognise the separation. At home, their reticence about what happens in school is equally determined, so that the sense of essential difference is strong. They generally do not want to talk about the experience of school at home and vice versa.

This reticence comes about because pupils know that they need to adapt. This necessitates politeness, as well as resilience. It means that they are unwilling to explore the issues that matter to them in the confines and expectations of school. Those things that are of most concern to them do not have a direct bearing on the experience of school. Sometimes the two overlap, but these are more likely to take place with peers than in formal lessons, in a volatile manoeuvres of the playground or the more private anguishes of tests and competition.

What pupils bring

The first day in any school is a juxtaposition between two worlds, two experiences and two sets of expectations. Whilst children quickly learn how to become pupils, how to be polite, how to fit, how to keep out of trouble, their personal lives continue in a kind of parallel world. What they bring with them, and the way they have learned so far might be ignored by the way that the school system operates but it is never forgotten by them.

Let us remind ourselves of the cast of mind of a young child. There are three aspects that are well known and well researched (Cullingford 2007, Damasio 2000). The first is children's capacity. The second is the way that they learn, and the third is the desire to know and understand.

Research on cognition demonstrates how powerful the mind is, not just as an instrument full of potential, but one in use from the beginning: analysing, discriminating and trying to find meaning. The problem for young children is that they are trying to find out for themselves, without support or instructions. They are bound to make idiosyncratic judgements for themselves since there is little external help. The tragedy is that this state of affairs continues throughout their youth, although the means of help have become available. We also know from the study of genetics how finely balanced is the role of nature and nurture, the latter being something we can deal with.

Given that young children are learning by and for themselves, without a language fully formed to categorise experience, they have to learn from context and from associations. They make their own connections between facts and ideas through observation, analysis and inference. They learn best by being able to share what they are thinking about someone else who could help them shape their ideas. This intellectual relationship is one in which both share their ideas about the matter in hand, whatever that matter happens to be. It is one of the reasons that stories play such a crucial part in young children's lives.

All this is a sparse reminder of research, but it does explain what children most need. Their capacity and their attempts to make sense of the world in which they so precipitately find themselves means that they have a deep yearning to understand. They do not only wish to know about their unique place but about their relationship to others. They want to understand people and not just themselves. They are quick to perceive that everyone has a separate point of view, and as early as we can trace a child's awareness of language we can see their acknowledgement of falsehood. The most sophisticated of social skills are acquired very early.

This means that young children have important questions to ask. They want to know about the meaning of life, about mutability, the idea of time and eternity, the size of the universe, and many imponderable matters. Most of all they want to know about people. Why do people behave as they do? Why is society so full of inequalities and the social world so full of contrasts? What motivates human action?

These are the essential matters that children want to explore. What do they then do with their desire to learn?

What pupils need

When one listens to young children, and hears what they say, not imposing on them ideas of what they ought to say but recognising their points of view, they make their wishes clear. These viewpoints raise questions about the extent to which their needs and wishes are met, and whether the system we take for granted is surely the best means of educating them. Meanwhile, we have an education system that is essentially unchanged for at least 150 years, and we are concerned with helping teachers cope.

The first need that children clarify is the recognition of their capacity. From the teacher's point of view, it is easy to see a disparity of ability amongst the pupils, as well as the differences in personality. This is a level of differentiation that does not go to the heart of the dilemma. Below individual differences lie deeper levels of the desire for understanding and while these will have been nourished in some and derided in others, this striving to understand is significant for them. To realise that pupils have important questions, and to realise at the same time that the ethos of school does not encourage time to deal with such questions, is a significant stance to take.

Many of the questions that children will ask are expressed in terms of ethics and of logic; ethical issues abound. There are two sites of contention in a school, and both are to do with discipline. One site is the playground, the corridors, the interplay between peers. This is where concern with bullying and unfairness is an expression not just of anger and bewilderment but genuine moral concern. The teacher can easily be placed in an almost impossible position of judge and jury (as well as police officer), but this is a starting point for insight into the pupils' dilemmas, and also a signal that the pupils themselves could be encouraged to address these issues openly, collectively and publicly.

The other site of concern is the general application of school rules, since pupils are aware of the distinction between those rules that are ethical and those that are a matter of convenience, between those that are created through the ease of administration, and those that are based on more fundamental principles. Rules can seem arbitrary as well as sensible. Pupils express their understanding of the need for rules but they also resent them when they are trivial or misapplied. The sense of social unfairness is based on seeing how arbitrarily some rules are enforced, rather like the legal system, based not so much on notions of justice, but on self-protection, where the most heinous crime is 'contempt of court'.

Recognition of the pupils' intellectual capacity is based on the knowledge that they are constantly thinking about issues of fairness and unfairness, rules and justice, and about their place in society. This should not be ignored. It is a tragedy that such questions have almost no part in the formal curriculum, a signal from which children learn a great deal. The capacity of children, all children, is revealed in their ability to employ logic, to question certain positions. It is the basis of intellectual development, a Socratic argument where the interplay of ideas is what counts rather than the imposition of will. We ask ourselves how often such rational conversations take place, even if pupils' ability to think critically at a high level is often proved (Quinn 1997).

Relationships

Logical dialogue depends on an iterative intellectual relationship. Just as children long to have their personal capacity and individual identity recognised, so they yearn for relationships. Recognition of personal interest is not a matter of testing, of displays of knowledge, of being good at doing set tasks, but an acknowledgement of individual concerns, of all the ideas and feelings they bring with them. The chance to learn new ideas and discuss them with someone else, especially with adults, is always relished and makes a deep impact. The subject matter itself is not as important as the curiosity and willingness to share ideas. Again, such a dialogue contrasts with the delivery of facts laid down by authority, to which the receiver has to submit. Whilst pupils assume that in the school system all questions are closed, they actually long for open questions.

The relationships that make such a strong impact are of a particular kind (Wells 1985, Richman *et al.* 1982). They do have to be warm and emotional or personally involving. They are intellectual dialogues about points of interest. They are like the conversations one has with someone interesting, even a passer-by, who will never be seen again. For adults, it is a stimulating and natural part of life (or ought to be). For pupils, it is a necessity.

The willingness to find time for conversation, for sharing a topic, is all that is required. Teachers are in the perfect position to do this, provided that they are not playing the role of teacher but that of an adult. Pupils appreciate this, since such conversations do not imply any favour or favouritism but simply the recognition that all have their own point of view, like an adult.

Language and logic

The old saying that people learn by doing is probably more true of adults than children. People have to learn for themselves in their own way, which explains how much research is a matter of 'reinventing the wheel'. Pupils learn faster, and they do so through language and its uses that include testing ideas. If we remind ourselves of young children's capacity to learn language, through analysis, in context, so that they make it their own, we see how important is the exploration of ideas through language.

Young children learn language by listening, detecting how it works, understanding it through the context in which it operates and by practising. They are never exactly 'taught' language. That is reserved for a second or third language, deliberately acquired. One does not need to go deeply into language acquisition and linguistics to see how subtle and complex the process is, or to acknowledge how much depends on practising. All language is learned by its need and by its use. Both can be fostered.

The kind of language that education requires is not just the language of emotional expression or those of wants. It is the language of definitions and distinctions. We know that there is a difference between the language used at home by children and that this makes a profound difference to their subsequent success or failure (Heath 1983). The linguistic skills demanded by academic challenges are different from those used everyday, and this can be encouraged.

The language that matters is not simply a matter of jargon, or lists of names for different groups of objects, from 'herds' to 'packs'. It is the language of argument. The employment of critical dialogue, of logic, of philosophy is not merely a sign of erudition but the strengthening of the mind. Given the capacity of pupils and their ability to master several new words in a day, the enrichment of vocabulary for the sake of putting it to use should be a priority. This means open questions and discussion. Pupils save their real intellectual arguments for each other, and learn a lot from them. This can be encouraged, but also fostered in the formal aspects of school.

Information shared

If pupils bring with them a sense of society and their place in it, as well as curiosity about moral values, they base this on experience and observation. They are aware of what they experience in their neighbourhoods, and what is presented to them on the news. Domestic or international disasters are not hidden from them. They know about politics and the controversies of the day. This means that they have an awareness of all the issues that are as worthy of discussion as they are of puzzlement.

Acknowledging that they all are, to some extent, aware of the news, of current events, of critical debates, leads to an acceptance and even encouragement that all will have a point of view. Tolerance, understanding other people and accepting differences are all based on the expression and sharing of ideas, rather than their suppression or assertion. It is a shame that controversial issues are eschewed for the sake of the accumulation of facts in the National Curriculum, since empirical evidence should be at the service of, rather than separated from, ideas. Just as pupils want to see the relevance of subjects in terms of the real world so they like to discuss matters of mutual interest. The subject matter itself does not matter. It can be quite trivial, like personal preferences, but any interest is a starting point for discussion, where informed opinions can be heard and where personal concerns strike a relationship with the formal curriculum.

What pupils receive

Pupils long for certain satisfactions and stimulations. Whether they expect them is another matter. As they make their way through the years of schooling towards the goal of the getting away from the experience of school, either out of or beyond, it becomes less easy to say 'pupils' and mean the majority. The demands of the curriculum, the organisation of schools and the awareness of the competition of tests and targets mean that many of the hopes of what schooling and learning could be like are very and too successfully overcome. This is not the teacher's fault, but the way in which the educational system is set up.

What children receive from school, to which they are made to adapt, is, essentially, the opposite of what they need. Their desires, especially in the early years, are clear, and they are equally clearly not met. Pupils' expressions of their school experiences are negative and laconic. They do think about it much since they have to submit to the experience. Only when they reflect on it and recall what they thought it could be like, do they begin to express a puzzled bewilderment and a sense of disenchantment. This is a general sense of the structures and systems which begins to permeate their ideas about individual teachers. The fact that teachers are associated closely with the organisation that they represent, means there is always a general barrier to understanding that teachers have to overcome.

It is an oft repeated joke that young children ask difficult, even impossible questions that we cannot answer, so we send them to school to learn not to ask questions. When pupils think about the delight of education, of learning, and the realities of schools, the juxtaposition between them is clear. But then, this is not something that is often thought about and certainly not encouraged to be thought about. The system seems implacable, and there is an atavistic sense that it should not be challenged, let alone changed.

Children come to school with a genuine desire to learn. Education, the process of understanding and discovery, of mastery of skills as well as the delight of employing them, the excitement of a new discovery, as well as the sharing of ideas; this is what life is for. Human beings have an instinctive awareness of language, but they also learn that language can be used for falsehood. They are natural researchers, observing systematically and empirically but they also learn that research can be corrupted. Young children come to school wanting to learn, but their experience is of being taught. Their open questions are met with closed ones. The desire to share ideas is discouraged for the sake of silence and individual writing. Their time is often spent in waiting: queuing and waiting to begin.

Observed from outside with a neutral eye, such enforced massing of young people, grouped together in front of monitors, engaged in rote activities without a deep sense of purpose beyond the fact that they have to be there, would strike anyone is anomalous. The ethos of schooling is so deeply embedded in the political culture that it is taken for granted, but if we look at it with the neutrality of the pupils' experience, rather than the imposition of policy by the inspectors, we should be allowed to recognise that something very strange is going on, and it is this reality that teachers attempt to overcome, or at least mitigate.

What pupils receive from school are some clear messages about what they have to accept. One is the hegemony of fact and matter that is supposed to be easily accumulated and more easily tested. The second is the organisation of groups, mostly large, all receiving the same message, preferably in silence. The third is the significance within these groups of personal competition, of hierarchies of success and failure, of being put in a certain position on a table. The fourth is the imposition of rules, an imposition because they, like all parts of school, do not arise out of agreement or discipline or good conduct but seem to be a given not to be questioned.

The power of facts

Pupils avoid talking about the formal aspects of school, but when they do one is confronted either by a moment that they remember as one of sudden and unique illumination or by a more general sense of doing subjects in a vague general routine. The former, great moments are rare, but the sense of underlying disparate subjects is pervasive. The pupils' impression of the curriculum is a dominance of two subjects, English and maths, a dominance confirmed by the timetable and the standard assessment tests.

It is not a dominance of the subjects themselves that strikes them as much as the mechanical way in which they are taken. There are repetitive routines. They know they are important but don't know why. If pressed to explain, their reasons repeat the circular argument that certain subjects dominate the timetable and the examination simply because the government says they are important. They have to accept this since they cannot escape them. What they talk about is not just boredom or a lack of a sense of intrinsic worth but a plethora of exercises and routines, of learning by rote. The feeling of purpose in the real sense passes them by. Subjects are a matter of being kept ostensibly busy, producing enough work on demand, neither too little nor too much, and keeping pace with the rest of the class.

When asked what they did at school the pupils will tend to say 'English and maths'. They will mention the routine of the subject rather than the interest of the content. They will think of the hours spent working quietly at a desk, producing work, only talking surreptitiously. This is the routine of school. The feeling is of its pervasive and familiar nature. They know there are 'subjects' in a hierarchy of importance, all of which they have to undergo. They might prefer some to others, but any personal interest or specialism, any sign of pursuing a line of knowledge seems to them forbidden.

There are tasks to be completed, facts to be remembered for tests. The idea that they might be pursuing knowledge for its own sake, or excited by original discoveries, or moved by the answers to questions, is replaced by their sense of the mechanical routines. Of course there are occasional moments of excitement, of an individual teacher's enthusiasm, but the general impression pupils give is of the need to keep their heads down, avoid trouble, and guess what is wanted. They learn to resent what is demanded of them. This impression is not because they cannot be bothered to elaborate on experience but because they find the experience so uniform. There is really little to say.

Nevertheless, this is what they are used to and what they accept. The formal experience of schools lies in carrying out set tasks. The excitements lie elsewhere. Sometimes the two overlap, but rarely are they brought together, as in collaborative learning. Whilst teachers will point out that there are many stratagems and new techniques they employ to heighten interest, the pupils still see the underlying sameness of the school's routines.

Groups of people

Learning is essentially a social activity. It is a matter of sharing other people's ideas, reacting to them, and a constant iterative dialogue. The odd thing about the experience of school is that it depends on groups, on pupils being brought together, in classrooms or around tables, but in this collective massing real collaboration plays a small part. It is as if people are brought together for them to ignore each other. The feeling is that there are many obedient individuals quietly and anonymously getting on with their work, despite the temptations of discussing and learning.

Schools create an ambivalent attitude towards learning. There are contradictions between the competition, the need of individuals to go it alone and prove themselves so that they alone are being tested, and the general assumption that collaborative learning is not a bad thing. The sharp end of the contradiction, however, is the way in which pupils understand learning as a social activity, and yet are taught that talking with others is disruptive. The tasks that pupils receive are a constant juxtaposition of group and individual work or, as often, individual work carried out in groups.

I like working in a group mostly, but it doesn't bother me working on my own. Because there's a lot more people there and you can find out other things from what they're doing. (girl, year 10)

In the group, because you can discuss it and because you get different opinions of what you're doing, don't you, and stuff about what you're doing. (boy, year 10)

The contradictory attitudes towards the stimulation that pupils receive from working with each other stems from the necessity of keeping control, for the disciplines of silence and order and from the fine line between constructive collaboration and the pleasure of talk. While we know that people learn at a vast variety of levels, and in many important ways from what seems like idle chatter, there is an assumption made with classrooms that all conversation should be 'on task', directed to the matter in hand. For pupils, this is a constraint that does not take sense. They feel that talking is useful, and that it can aid learning. They do not make such a distinction between the kind of talk that is allowed for answering questions, and that which is disapproved. For pupils, both kinds of talk can support learning, but one is more pleasurable than the other.

For the pupils, group work means the opportunity to talk to each other.

You get more ideas, tell other people what you feel, and they can tell you what they feel. (boy, year 10)

When you work in a group you don't have to do it by yourself. If you're working in threes, a person can to do all that and the person can do the other thing and you can get it done quicker. (girl, year 10)

So we can co-operate together instead of all on your own, you might get stuck if you've got no one to talk to. If you're in a group, everyone's together. You can help each other. (boy, year 10)

Whilst the arguments for collaboration seem to the pupils irrefutable, the sense that they have tasks to carry out prevails. Because of this distinction between the pleasures of conversation and the utility of support from peers more importance is placed on the usual and expected tasks.

Talking is associated with noise, with disruption. It also interferes with the steady concentration on individual work, producing writing or answers that can be inspected. The prevailing assumption is that a well-run classroom is silent, with everyone working by him- or herself except in particular conditions. While pupils relish the idea of collaborating, of sharing ideas and while iterative conversations are the mainstays of learning, they are aware that talking is associated in schools with disruption, with activities that undermine the steady concentration of writing. Collaboration is itself contrary to the essential task of competition.

Competition

Pupils are constantly tested; they also test each other. They are made aware of where they are placed in rank order, whether in clubs, institutions or individuals, as if it were an essential attribute of the culture in which they find themselves. Whilst they are aware of the general disparity between people in society, between the rich and poor, the celebrities and the rest of us, the more immediate experience is of the constant challenge at least to keep up with the others. Whilst there are many who find it easier to avoid the discontent of not succeeding, there are many ways in which they are expected to do well. They know there is a kind of competition against each other and for the teachers' awareness. Competition is not a matter of playing games or enjoying the challenge but a far more prosaic anxiety of whether they are doing well enough.

> They just might be a bit cleverer than me. And if they're getting things quicker than me, they're going to be cleverer than me. If they get it quicker than you, or they finish it. Sometimes when I do my work quickly, I'm really bored afterwards. So you finish slowly, you won't be bored. (girl, age 8)

The secret of a successful, quiet school career is to do well enough, to keep up with the norms. If too much is done the danger is that you would be accused of being too clever or 'posh', 'because you would be called brainy and perfect' (girl, age 8). Their often repeated fear is encapsulated in the phrase, 'do it again' so everything has to be done carefully to fit in to the teachers' expectations and to remain quiet.

> Some people whisper to me and that, and I just whisper back and they keep carry on doing it. And I just keep on doing it. I don't get my work done. Sometimes she says, like, 'that's not a lot, is it?' and things like that. It's quite hard and that and the teachers helping somebody else. Like helping another person who gets there before me and I get a bit annoyed about that as well. (boy, age 8)

Pupils are aware of the norms of expectations, not just of each other but the demands of the teacher. To them, this depends more on the amount produced, rather than the quality. Pupils realise that they are expected to produce lots of work, to be seen to be busy and attentive. Keeping up means getting the work done on time, and this entails being acutely aware of how the other pupils are doing.

> Sometimes when you're doing maths things, you will have to do it quietly, sit on your own with books around you, so no one will copy you and you can't copy them. I start sweating and feel 'oh, I'm not going to be able to do this and

everyone is going to finish before me' and things like that. Whoever is the best in the classes is usually the bossiest and everyone doesn't like you very much. (girl, age 8)

When work becomes a chore and something to be calculated against other people's expectations, it is difficult to do really well. The fear of not keeping up does not foster that creative impulse that always strives to something better but instead gives a sense of standardisation, of doing enough lest other people should complain. The awareness of other pupils is not so much what they are doing, for that would be a form of collaboration, but how much they are producing. The need to make sure that no one sees your work whilst you are writing it is not because they might learn something, but that they might copy.

The temptation of copying is a telling insight into school. It is a shortcut. It avoids doing meaningless things. If there were a striving to learn then this form of cheating would not arise. It is a quick way of fulfilling set tasks, and that is how pupils tend to see the work of schools.

Most of the time you're only copying from books and you learn nothing. You don't learn nothing (sic). Or they give you a textbook, two add three you write it down. It's simple 'cause you're just copying. (boy, age 8)

Copying is part of the routines of school, as long as it is copying from a textbook. Copying from other pupils' work is considered utterly different as it goes against the individualistic norms of schooling. The pupils learn not just about these rules and regulations which are clear to them but about their anomalies. They understand that what matters is the work that they as individuals produced quietly by themselves. But they also know that the whole system is based on competition.

The rules

Many of the rules that govern schools are implicit. They consist of shared beliefs and assumptions. While they can be made explicit, rules do not always make sense to the pupils. They seem arbitrary, a matter of whim, rather than anything thought out. One obvious example is that of clothes, of uniform or of standards when the line between what is acceptable and what is considered deviant is very fine, especially given that such matters are constantly being tested. It is at this level of decision that authority imposed on others and that the rules in school are interpreted.

Because you can't do anything without being tagged by anyone. If you go one way you get done. If you go around to the front of the school, you get done. If you go round the back you get done. If you go to the side, you'll get done. (boy, year 10)

It is as if rules were interpreted as an excuse for 'getting done'. Pupils assume that behaviours that are easily detectable, visible and easy to measure are what is under scrutiny, rather than motivation or more complex behaviour.

The restrictions of school are received in many ways. The rules against talking or too much help being given to each other, of producing certain quantities of work overlap with the rules about space, where they are allowed to go. The school is not just a physical entity, but full of barriers. There is no freedom of movement. The essential constraint is that pupils are ordered to certain places at certain times.

Not really good. There is nothing to do. There are certain areas where you're allowed and certain areas where you are not and there is nothing to keep you occupied. When you have the TV you are not allowed to watch in certain classrooms. (girl, year 10)

Rules that they've made. Like they say this place is out of bounds and all that stuff and they make it as if it were a prison or something. (girl, year 10)

There are different levels of rules. The most powerful are the implicit norms of behaviour, those matters that need to be learned by guesswork and by emulating others. The real ethos of school depends on the collective understanding of what is expected, on conformity, on submitting to the demands. The fact that many of these rules do not have rational grounds or are not explained does not help.

What pupils observe

Much of what pupils learn at school does not depend on or derive from the tasks they undergo or the facts that are given to them. They learn through observation. Whilst these are not matters that are formally tested, the subject matter of these experiences is of profound importance. Pupils look at the ways that people behave. They see this in the rituals of the classroom and in the behaviours of the playground. Their understanding of the way that society operates is based not on what they are told but on the interactions between people. They observe both the formal structure of hierarchies and the informal organisation of power.

In the ritualistic arrangement of school, the assemblies, the register, the repetition of routine and the language which is deployed, the pupils observe the organisation of control. They understand who wields power and where this comes from. They know the effects of inspection and are aware which teachers have real command and which do not. They observe the formal living society, the need for the manipulation of behaviour from rules, and the placing of people into different groupings where the group is more important than the individual (Measor and Woods 1984).

They also observe the informal behaviour of groups in the playground, and the way in which individuals can be coerced by gangs into certain kinds of behaviours. They also witness the way in which some are coerced into silence, or the way in which pupils become willing accomplices by remaining silent and uninvolved. All pupils see bullying. It is not a rare occurrence or one that only affects a few but is a pervasive part of school life, unfortunately. One should not pretend it is otherwise since all the pupils will talk about the experiences that they have had, both as victims and bullies. They make it quite clear that all forms of teasing and provocation take place. They know how to provoke and are aware of provocation. The bullying does not have to be physical to be effective. Teasing, being ignored, being 'picked on' or despised is part of the emotional atmosphere of school (Besag 1989, Cullingford 1991).

> If only people wouldn't come up to me and start kicking me and that. When they start, if I can catch them I just get up and swing them around because I get so annoyed with them. They do it to some people and call them names like really horrible names. (boy, age 8)

> Sometimes I push people over by accident, and they said I did it on purpose so I get annoyed. And sometimes I get in trouble and I say 'that's not fair!' and things like that and I think I shouldn't do that and I can't stop myself as they push me over as well, sometimes. (girl, age 7)

Bullying is subtle and pervasive, an significant if inadvertent part of school life and teachers need to be aware of this and deplore, rather than ignore, the situation. Through the constant internecine strife, the pupils are learning essential ideas about what they can get away with and about the pleasures of inflicting pain on others. They learn about the power of gangs and the need for mutual support. All this learning is unstructured but it is intense. It is not only a matter of testing friendships and exploring relationships, but knowing how people behave, the reasons for this, both good and bad, and how to position themselves so they can choose how deeply to be involved. Just as they keep their heads down in lessons, so they acquire the habit of keeping away from trouble and of knowing how to remain uninvolved.

As pupils look back on their experience of school, they summarise what appears to them as a prevailing atmosphere.

> There were quite a lot of fights…About people calling each other names … People nicking pencils off each other, just childish things really. (girl, age 16)

> When you see someone bullying people I don't like that. I normally fight for that as well. There was a lot in school. They used to just get bullied, just name-calling. (boy, age 18)

As pupils get older, the social life of the school becomes more and more important for them. The meeting place of friends and enemies, the school is a certain kind of society and a glimpse into social behaviour. It is a microcosm of what will continue to be experienced in later life. Whether such turbulent experiences need to be prepared for in this way is a moot point but, although the social world of peer-group influences and exchanges is influential, such insight takes place in a peculiar context.

Looking back on the experience of school, pupils are aware of the contrast between the ragged, informal and disorganised life outside classrooms and the otherwise detailed rituals of control in which these turbulent experiences are covered up or ignored. Whilst the unofficial life of school is more and more significant, the old routines continue.

> Getting detentions and having to get there early in the morning. (girl, age 16)

> Just writing essays and stuff like that. I didn't really like it. The comprehension where you just had to read questions and read passages out. (boy, age 16)

It is the concurrence of what seems meaningless and unnecessary together with a volatile reaction to peer-group pressure that cause some to turn obviously away from school. Others, whilst feeling psychologically excluded, still preserve a sense of submission to the rituals of school.

However quietly the pupils appear to adapt, they are nevertheless observing. Those questions that concern them when they are young – why do people behave in the way they do – still trouble them but these are not dealt with formally. Instead, pupils try to work out for themselves their attitudes and judgements about human behaviour and their own reactions to it. They receive clear messages about what is expected of them. On one level is the formal sense of control and reward.

> Suppose people do a good piece of work, and they get a commendation slip, which sort of like commends them for their work and after you get so many of these commendation slips you get a commendation slips certificate, but lately people have just been going into lessons behaving for say nine of them and disrupting the rest of the year. And because they have behaved for those nine the teacher sees this as a surprise and he commends them with commendation slips. (boy, age 10)

It is the first hint of some kind of purpose in school that underlies the expectations. There are rewards and punishments. While the latter seems often arbitrary and piecemeal, based not on true judgement or agreed moralities but on small details and arcane whims, so the idea of rewards, of commendations and gold stars, systems of badgering and labelling with medals, appears to pupils, as they grow older, to be essentially flawed. They might to start to accept the excitement of such palpable and public praise, but they soon realise that it is part of a system of control.

What pupils observe are the devices used to organise them, subdue them and prepare them for set tasks. They know that there are many sanctions used to control them, and that the system is based on the assumption that at least some of them, if not all, go unwillingly into the regime of school. Pupils connect their personal experience with the observations of society. They are aware of the hierarchies and control mechanisms of school, including rewards and particularly punishment, and connect these to those of society as a whole. They see the prison system, the need to catch and incarcerate criminals as a means through which a recalcitrant and dissident, as well as a disenfranchised, society is kept in some kind of order.

Pupils are aware of government policy through the media, their parents and their peers. It is important to be aware of the fact that targets, league tables and the inspection system, closures, special measures and other comparisons and punishments are not hidden from the pupils. They know about academies, Beacon Schools, sink schools and 'bog standard' comprehensives, as well as private schools and league tables of universities. To pretend that pupils are unaware of this is impossible for anyone who talks to them but it sometimes feels as if government policy is based on the idea of pupils' unawareness of what is going on. The impact of what they observe in school is so strong because it connects to their observation of the wider world.

What pupils observe in school is a peculiar snapshot of society, one in which control is central with its rewards and punishments and where the idea that controls are necessary because no one wants to be there, goes deeper. They observe the different levels of control in a series of hierarchies in which some figures are shadowy and others occasional. But this gives them a very definite interpretation how societies operate. They extrapolate from their experience, as well as from their knowledge, their expectations of themselves.

What pupils experience in school

There are many excitements in school, mostly unexpected and inadvertent and all the more interesting because they contrast with the general routines. The overall impression that pupils have of school, however, is the way in which the same things happen again and again. There might be some days that are better than others, but the experience is dominated by the rituals of routine from registration to the ceremony of the ending of the day. The better or worse days depend on what lessons take place at particular times and Friday might always be everyone's favourite but the differences are marginal. Every day the curriculum is similar, dominated by English and mathematics. Although there are the significant periods of time spent in the playground and social activities, the bulk of time is spent queuing and waiting for something to happen or sitting at the desk (the computer still takes up a small proportion of the time) (Cullingford and Haq 2009).

Allowing for the moments of pleasure and the satisfaction of learning and carrying out a successful task, the pupils, in the analysis of the experience of school, stress the routines. It is not only the psychologically excluded who complain about the amount of boredom. It is a central part of the school experience. All pupils talk about having to do tasks that they find meaningless and boring. They are given exercises, sheets to copy out. Despite being accepted as a necessary part of schooling and justifiable this still strikes pupils as dull at best, and at worst appears to be given to keep them occupied, and silent.

At one level, this system is taken for granted. It can hardly be denied. It is held to be a necessary part of learning, without which the pupils would be left without skills or knowledge. But is it justified? Has it proved to be efficacious? From the pupils' point of view, many of the tasks remain simply boring and they do not think they gain anything by doing them. They also feel that these tasks are imposed for the wrong reasons and that their primary response must be to keep their head down and stay out of trouble. This desire to be invisible and unnoticed can be a result of not understanding.

> Some of the teachers, they tend to view textbooks, take it from there. It's quite boring. (girl, age 11)

> I didn't like the writing. I just used to find it really boring. I just couldn't be bothered. All the others used to be there writing and I couldn't. I started not bothering going. (woman, age 21).

> Most of the time you're only copying from books and you learn nothing, you learn just nothing. What they give you is a textbook. They give you…lower work. (man, age 21)

Those pupils who reflect on their overall experience of school mention the mixture of routines and boredom, the repetition of meaningless tasks. Those who do not manage to survive the experience mention the disruption from others. They talk about having to alleviate the boredom by finding an alternative source of interest. But whilst those who have had the most negative experiences are the most vehement, and those who feel they have failed are the most bitter, the experience of boredom is pervasive.

It's a bit boring at times. There's nothing to do. It's boring. Usually we sit in the form room and talk. (girl, year 10)

There's not very much to do. It is quite boring. (boy, year 10)

Part of the sense of having nothing to do derives from the ethos of school, that it depends on instructions and on the control by teachers. Pupils are not assumed to learn by themselves. If left to their own devices, after all the ways in which they had been trained, they will not know what to do. There's no sense of constructive learning, of natural, individual initiative. The boredom is a result of reliance on imposition at one moment and emptiness at the next when they are released from the pressure of enforcement. The structure of school life rests on a clear demarcation between lessons and playground, to the diminution of both.

When pupils have little to do and are not fully occupied, they find themselves waiting for something to happen. Waiting is itself a central ritual of schooling.

Most of the time is spent just hanging around, talking to your friends. (girl, year 10)

When the curriculum is so organised, and there are set tasks as well as set tests, the contrast between the demands of concentration in the classroom and the release from it will seem clear. The sense of waiting, of hanging around also pervades the classroom where pupils are doing similar tasks at their own pace. The opportunity to do nothing, provided one is not disrupting, is often taken up, preparing the writing materials, ostensibly thinking. The problem is that if the work is dull there will automatically be time wasting, a sense of tedium. It is the sense of routine that causes disaffection.

Like if you have spellings at the end of the week you get 10 spellings on Monday and on a Friday you have to read them out. (girl, age 8)

This might be a necessary imposition of standards and expectations, but tests are rarely interpreted as beneficial or purposeful. They are linked to routines and to tedium. The very activities that should be stimulating can become repetitive and meaningless.

...Used to walk in the classroom, and maybe people sat with faces long and, like all in their own little worlds. Then some of them will be doing stupid things you think, 'God, please get me out.' (female, age 20)

Those moments of reflection, questioning the purpose of what takes place is naturally most apparent in the disaffected, but it affects all. Even the most dedicated pupil knows the drudgery of the boring lesson, of trying to do a task that is not understood. Most simply submit to the conditions. There are chores to be done, not necessary but imposed. There is a need to be patient, knowing that time will inevitably pass. Those who accept rather than rage against the conditions have a laconic attitude.

> It seems all right … Some bits have been all right, but some years have not been all right. They weren't listening to me. (girl, year 10)

'It's all right' is the language of submission, of knowing the need to accept the conditions. For the pupils there is a sense that many of the tasks given to them are repetitions. They'd been done before, and are at best dull. Many of the said tasks also appear to be meaningless, without a clear goal beyond keeping a class busy and quiet. Keeping pupils occupied is not what teachers want but is a consequence of the National Curriculum and the way it is designed, with targets, the same content for all and insistence on coverage rather than relevance. When people look back on their experience, they recall the amount of time spent 'copying'.

> Just writing essays, and stuff like that, but I didn't really like it. The comprehension, where you just had to read questions and read passages out. I didn't really take much interest. I found it harder to learn in that kind of way rather than just happen to be in the class and having to do the work. (boy, age 19)

> I didn't like the paperwork. Half the time you're messing about … don't learn much. I used to just sit in the classroom. (woman, age 21)

The most telling comment that explains the sense of routine and repetition, not depending on the dislike of a particular subject, but the nature of schooling, is a sense of it all having no purpose, of being essentially meaningless in terms of learning.

> As long as you get your work done, it's all right, and your voice isn't too high but some of the stuff I don't see any point in doing. I don't really see the need. It's pointless. It's all right; basically, you just get sheets and fill them in. It's really boring and pointless. I mean there's no point in writing it down. (girl, year 10)

Whilst the phrase 'it's all right' symbolises the acceptance of doing repetitive work because that is what always happens. The phrase that is associated most closely with the tasks of school is 'do it again'. Neat work, well presented, that demonstrates that time has been spent – if not necessarily anything learned – appears to be the goal.

Pupils' experiences of school are conditioned by the absence of an explicit sense of purpose. Much of the work is meaningless not because they cannot see the point of it, but because it appears to be done for its own sake. The routines, the rote learning, the copying and the repetitions are all nourished by the sense that they are being given out to keep things going, to keep the pupils occupied. In the absence of an explicit purpose pupils extrapolate what the purpose might be from policy announcements, and the occasional mission statement, and from the way in which the school functions.

Pupils know that there are statutory orders, and that they must go to school. They know that the outcome is their employability and their future lives. If this were made clear, then the whole of the curriculum and the ethos of working would be to this end. But it is not so. The school is not supposed to be focused simply on employable skills. It has other contradictory tasks, like the academic prowess of its pupils and their social education. The kind of purpose pupils look for is their own understanding, and the conduct of people. If there were a clear vision of what the whole exercise is for, then the experience would be quite different. The sense of having to submit, of saying at best 'it's all right' is due not only to the daily experiences of school and its routines, but the lack of any personal sense of purpose. It is all very well to have a hierarchy of exams to pass, and pupils are well aware of the need to do well to progress, but they are also aware of the dominance of English and maths, subjects assumed to be central but which are rarely made interesting. They are done because they have to be done.

It is a pity that pupils rarely sense that the purpose of schooling is spelled out or discussed. Perhaps this is because any purpose needs to be made personal and this is not how schools operate. Perhaps it is because schools have no real or clear purpose beyond meeting policy requirements and the demands of competitiveness. When pupils are asked about why they are in school it is clear that the experience is not valued in itself. It is what happens afterwards that counts. In contrast with universities where the sense of the opportunity of being there is all important, for pupils in school it is an experience that has to be undergone to emerge from a rite of passage. Afterwards, people talk of 'the best years of their lives', but that is not what it feels like at the time, apart from some to whom it is a comparatively safe and undemanding place.

Pupils are, however, aware of the importance of the hidden curriculum, which is centred on the social aspects of school, the interaction with peers and the observation of behaviour. That the essential aspects of pupils' lives should be officially marginalised by the set curriculum explains why the routine experiences of the classroom tend to mean so much less than they should.

The obvious answer about the purpose of school is to get a job, but pupils rarely recalled even having this made explicit for them. One girl typically recalls an attempt by her school to clarify its purpose.

I think we once, a couple of times they've taken us into the hall and the teacher spoke to all of us and said, like you've got to buck your ideas up because you're going to work, and they just really told us that it were about working, get education to go to work. And get through life. (girl, age 16)

The message really is about getting on with the tasks at hand. The idea of personal involvement, of individual outcomes is secondary. What pupils are left with is the sense of immediate routines.

Most of them never really bothered with purpose, because they concentrated more on just getting a lesson over and done with, getting one lesson after another all the way. Rarely, to try to get on with you. (boy, age 17)

If you do what they want you to do they don't bother talking to you. I don't think they tend to spend a lot of time with people who just get on with it. (girl, age 17)

How pupils cope

There are a number of ways in which pupils learn how to cope with the demands of school and emerge with their resilience intact:

1. *By guessing what is wanted.* Guessing, anticipating the demands, can sometimes replace any kind of thinking. The complexities of thought are developed through working out what they are supposed to do, what is in the teacher's mind, what the demands of the curriculum have to be. It seems that guessing right is essential because the alternative is so humiliating.
2. *By adapting to whatever the requirements are.* Having guessed and guessed correctly how they are supposed to behave, they accept the routines and settle into them. This is why they do not try to question too much what goes on, because that causes difficulties. Some of the most intelligent are the most disaffected because there is such a difference between the desire to learn and the actual experience of being taught. So pupils learn to adapt themselves, suppress questions, dismiss puzzlement and assume that it is all that they can expect.
3. *By deflecting their attention away from what interests them into other things.* To be able to survive in the classroom, as well as the playground, is to learn to deflect criticism, to avoid conflicts, to make certain that just enough is done to a prevent too much attention being paid to you. That is how protection can become a kind of survival. It is a way of laying blame on somebody else, and rejoicing in somebody else's problems. You are no longer 'on your own'. Deflection is way of avoiding being 'picked on' whether it is by other pupils or by teachers.
4. *By hiding.* They remain as invisible as possible. They don't want to do too much or they will be seen as being 'posh' or a 'snob' or being too clever. They must not

do too little, or they will be exposed. Instead, the very routines that schools offer are what pupils use to hide in the hope of being unnoticed, doing enough not to draw attention to themselves.

5. *By learning how to conform.* They know how to fit in, how to be quiet, how not to draw attention to themselves. It is contrary to the idea of confidence, of exploration, to the excitement of learning, but this is how pupils cope with the everyday life of school. They might not like to conform and some rebel against it but most just submit to the idea of conformity.

Pupils' resilience is admirable, but this also means that they are learning much that is bad, as well as much that is good. Resilience is a way of surviving despite what is going on, but it does not always bring the best out of people. What pupils learn in school are not those things that we would ideally expect them to learn. Teachers must be aware of this; it is the only way in which the honour of doing as good a job as possible can be met.

5

What pupils think of teachers

Teachers need to remind themselves constantly that pupils like to learn, but they resent being taught. This sums up the dilemma of teaching. There is an ambiguity between the person who is there to help, to share with and to talk to, and the role of 'delivering' a curriculum to a large group. The tensions are between the group and the individual, natural curiosity and an ordered series of subjects, as well as between the role and the personality of the teacher.

When teachers are struggling to cope, to come to terms with the conflicting demands that are made on them, it is this tension between the necessity to play a role and the individuality of the person that pupils see as most significant. The tension is exacerbated by the centralised control of the curriculum, the enforcement through inspection, and the targets and league tables. It is also made more difficult by the additional burdens that teachers have to carry, the paperwork, the demonstration for others of what is taking place, as well as the demands of having to deal with thirty individuals at the same time. It must be remembered, however, that while the difficulties for teachers are made far more extreme by the pervasive politics of control and accountability, the root of the problem goes far deeper. It is this that pupils detect: the essential ambiguity of a person placed in a circumstance like a school where the minority of privilege, however well-founded that privilege might be, control a far larger majority.

When pupils reflect on society they draw out many lessons from the experience of school. They know their place. They are led to assume that all the rules, the etiquettes, the expectations and the tasks are carried out for the sake of the teachers and for their convenience. Pupils conclude that they are not really the centre of the school, not the school's real purpose. The school is interpreted as being organised for the sake of teachers. The way in which rules are experienced and the very functioning of the school not only depends on the teachers and their duties but is seen as a symbol of the larger society, where the many have no real voice.

That feeling of comparative disenfranchisement enters deeply into the experience of school. All questions, however innocent, tend to be interpreted as closed questions, to which there is only one right answer. Even the most casual of inquiries can elicit a response such as, 'Why does she ask me that? What is she after?' Guessing what the teacher requires tends to replace normal processes of thought. The task in school is to find out what is expected and carry out such tasks as required, having found out what they are. Interpretation of the expectations of the rules is essential. It is a type of guessing game into which pupils are rarely privileged to participate. The school is a closed society, carefully controlled, and one in which there is always an element of force. Those studies that follow the experience of pupils are often surprised at how pervasive, if latent, is the spirit of revolt as if there were always the possibility of an uprising, by individuals or by groups.

Teachers will be the last to think of themselves as oppressors, but there is an element of this in the way that pupils see them. It is not how pupils would like to see them, but it is also accepted as a necessary part of the role. The teacher is there to command. This is nothing to do with personality but a function of their position. Pupils accept this fact as readily as they learn to regret it. The problems of discipline tend to come when the balance of role or personality on one side is exaggerated.

The teacher who uses the power of the impersonal role has the advantage of discipline, but it is a certain use of personality that makes him effective. Sometimes the power of command becomes attractive in itself, but it is unfortunate that without some ability to understand how this functions, teaching can be very difficult. From the pupils' point of view, however, the exaggerated role of teacher can prove problematic. They recognise and respect the ability to keep order, however absurd or unnatural such demands might be. They recognise that it is necessary in the particular conditions of the school, and yet they always long for a more personal contact, the ability to share a joke and see the human side of the individual. Given that they long for an iterative intellectual relationship with an adult, they are bound to want something more than the impersonal. One of the deepest regrets on leaving school is that they did not have the chance to know their teachers better (Cullingford 2002). The conditions do not readily allow it.

If pupils do not want the teacher merely to remain a role, neither do they want the teacher to lose all authority of purpose. Nothing is more despised than the teacher who is desperately trying to be liked, attempting to win favours. Pupils resent changes of mood, signs of emotional insecurity and attempts to cajole them into giving pity or affection. Pupils want there to be an acceptance that the teacher has a role to play but if the role is played too hard this can lead to difficulties, especially for those pupils who take everything personally and who are easily provoked. The balance of role and personality needs to be recognised.

As the power of the staff can be seen as an imposition and even become a battle of wills, a certain amount of authority is always expected. It is the authority of accepting a role and doing so with integrity. Any pretence is resented, which explains why the weakness of pleading or ineffective instructions is also disliked. It is, of course, a peculiar position for anyone to find themselves in, to have to command recalcitrant people to force them to obey. Is this also an idea of society that pupils acquire? That there is so much disquiet and resentment in schools ought to give people pause.

If the experience of school was pleasurable and geared to the pupils' needs then all teachers would have a very different role. We need to be aware, however, of the structural problems in the schooling system. The best schools put learning and values first despite the requirements of the National Curriculum. From the pupils' point of view, however, schools will always remain peculiar places, unnatural in the organisation of groups, in competition and in social display.

Whatever the ethos of the school, the teacher needs to retain a strong sense of integrity, of simply doing his or her best. The pupils appreciate that. They like the sense of the personal anecdote and the shared experience, the humour and the attention to detail. They accept this within the framework of what the school demands. Outside the school other intellectual relationships can be made. Within school, those moments of contact are rare.

The place of teachers

It is important to see teachers from the pupils' point of view and understand the conditions in which both work. It is not the tokenism of using pupils to help them adapt to the conditions. The pupils have more to say than simply trying to guess what they are supposed to do. They see the personalities involved and the structural position. They study the behaviour of teachers all the time, detecting and needing to work out how they might react. Whilst the majority keep quietly working there are always those who like to share jokes with the teacher, to see how far they can go. All appreciate humour as a sign of interest, but this is not of the humour that tries to draw attention to itself. It is the humour that is concerned in sharing understanding.

Pupils closely observe the peculiar demands on teachers, all the contradictions between duty and interest, role and concern. The very conditions in which teachers work and the way that pupils are organised seem to the pupils anomalous even if it becomes routine.

> Most of the schools I've been to, they have all this place, like units, you know what I am about, units of the stupid people. They should have more classrooms in schools, separate classrooms, where you have like three teachers between about ten pupils and see when you go to school. You have one teacher between so many pupils in the classroom. (man, age 20)

The very structure of classrooms, with one person commanding the work and behaviour of a large number, shows how little schools have changed their approach since the Lancasterian system of monitors. Whatever the size of the class, whatever the organisation, pupils cannot receive much individual attention. This has clear consequences like the unification of learning, like the drilling of ideas, a kind of collectivisation of the system. One consequence is that the teacher is placed in an exposed position.

> All he does is stand at the top of the classroom, shouts out this and that and the other and most of the time you're only copying from books and you learn nothing, you don't learn nothing. Or they give you a textbook, two and three, you write it down. It's simple, because you're just copying. (man, age 20)

From the pupils' perspective, the drudgery of copying and a feeling of meaninglessness puts the teacher at a distance. There's something absurd about the position. From the teacher's point of view, the demands on time, and the number of pupils as well as the set curriculum make it impossible to do much more than survive. The problem is that this seems like a weakness, as if the teacher were playing an inadequate or unworthy role. What the pupils look for is individual attention, dialogue and interesting tasks with a purpose. They do not always get it, not because of the teachers but because of the position in which they are placed.

> Those that aren't interested in work, because they're not getting the attention they need, there should be teachers there to give the attention they need. (man, age 20)

In the circumstances this is very difficult. The pupils recognise that they are there to learn but begin to wonder if that is really the purpose of schooling, rather than keeping them quiet and occupied.

> They give you like, lower work, like the younger people, and then from there you'll start working up, instead of letting you learn the proper stuff, like the hard work. They were just giving you easy work, what you could do and you were learning nothing. (woman, age 20)

There are some pupils who are frustrated at their own inability and lack of understanding but the complaints of the majority are that the work is simply not interesting and without context. The pupils want to be in engaged in ideas, they want demanding work and they long for the specific interest of teachers.

It is the circumstances, the context of work, that dominates, with classes split between those for whom the work is easy and those labelled (by pupils) as 'just a dunce'. The emphasis is on labelling, on being placed into groups rather than learning. In such a regime work is associated with being occupied and the complaints about the lack of demand centre on the meaningless routines.

The problem is that the teachers bear the brunt of criticism. In the circumstances of the school the teacher has a delicate task and can be up against recalcitrant, unwilling pupils. This seems an inevitable consequence of the way that schools function. On one level, this is absurd that someone who is there to help others to learn and fulfil themselves could have to act like a prison warden. But there is always an element of this and pupils observe how their teachers cope, to see how determined they are to overcome the problem.

> I wish the teachers were better. Some of them can't even control the class and you know, one teacher is actually frightened of this boy. Yes, he was. The teacher [was] just like 'all right do whatever you want'. (girl, year 11)

In these difficult circumstances pupils themselves want to give up, and they assume that teachers do as well. In the ideal case of the excitement of shared learning the teacher brings out the potential of the pupils and there is a strong sense of purpose. This can easily be eroded. Whilst there are many schools in which pupils bring with them negative attitudes, sometimes fostered by their parents, all schools are liable to be affected by the contagion of indifference. It is an attitude that quickly spreads; what is the point of it all? What is the purpose? Pupils are very easily cajoled into feeling that it is better to be 'cool', to be negative, to join in the general and seemingly fashionable idea that the whole experience is a waste of time. Nothing is more difficult for teachers than to be placed into a position where they are supposed to force pupils to do things.

Students long for those teachers who continue to care for them, and so whilst they themselves are prone to give up, they still resent it if a teacher seems to submit to the same lack of commitment.

> The teachers; it's just … I can't understand the point of view, they can't be bothered with it anymore, because like I say most of the people were just turning up at school because they had to; they didn't have to do any work when they were there. Teachers weren't basically there to teach them, they were there just to look after them basically. It's rather pointless if you're doing that. Some teachers were still trying to discipline them in the fifth year but other teachers just gave up. It was a lost cause. (boy, age 18)

Once a position has been reached in which the primary necessity is to control and keep order, and once there is a sense of opposition and a battle of wills, then the whole sense of purpose is lost. Yet teachers are constantly put in the position of keeping order and forcing pupils to do things. It is telling that this is rarely fundamentally questioned. I used to be proud of being able to instil discipline into the toughest inner-city boys, but I now wonder about this. Is there not something fundamentally wrong in such a system?

In such circumstances, when the pupils have long given up, it is easy for the teacher to do so, too. It is, however, a telling insight that the pupils still resent the fact; they remain committed enough to blame.

> Most of them at my school just never really bothered. The concentrated more on just getting the lesson over and done with, getting one lesson after another all the way really instead of trying to get on with you. (boy, age 17)

The hint of regret, of yearning for someone to get on with, contrasts with the sense of routine, in getting through the lessons, in surviving another school day.

When the teacher's role is displaced by the need to maintain order, the idea of education is diverted into battle of wills. This battle is dominated by the more vociferous pupils, the ones who do not simply submit. The irony is that the pupils' desire for individual attention is replaced by all the attention being placed on those least willing to learn.

> I don't think they tend to spend a lot of time with people who just get on with it and do whatever they want. You know, it's like all the people who don't tend to behave. They are the ones who get talking to all the time. So, if you do what they want you to do they don't bother talking to you really. (girl, age 17)

Given some of the difficulties that teachers have to face, one wonders why they do bother. The problem is that the unenviable position that teachers can find themselves in derives from the suspicion that pupils have about them, as if teachers were their enemies rather than their friends. The compulsory nature of the education system, not just in terms of attendance but modes of behaviour, means that teachers are distanced from the pupils. Instead of the assumption that the motivation must be there, or they would not try so hard, teachers are seen as part of a system and not only as individuals. One of the effects of the inspection system and the many public announcements about failing schools is that pupils see the way that teachers are controlled. They are told what to teach and how to teach. This is enforced by inspectors. Do Ofsted and other external agencies hold the real power? Teachers are assumed to be trying to get pupils to work, not because they care but because they are afraid of inspectors.

That sense of mutual trust and understanding, so longed for by pupils, is undermined by the system of inspectorial control and the doctrine of 'accountability'. The pupils, at least in part, see teachers as conforming to other people's wishes, fearful of external criticism, motivated by the dread of not doing well. The competition that pupils know about when applied to them, is also detected between teachers, and also between schools. The teachers are perceived as part of the system, alien, controlling everything and on the same side as those who run the system. At the same time, teachers remain individually of the greatest importance to pupils, so the pleasures of mutual understanding take place in a peculiar context.

The suspicions of teachers derive from the assumption that they have their own separate scenarios and alternate motivations.

> I didn't really speak much to teachers. I normally just get on with my work and stuff. To be honest, I didn't communicate very well with teachers, like I communicate better with my fellow pupils, more my age group. (boy, age 17)

One of the main points about teaching is the dialogue, the discussion that can be had. It is not a question of giving entertaining lectures, but sharing excitement, and discovering new ideas. Whilst all pupils long for good communication with disinterested adults there is also a tendency to see teachers as separate, doing what they are supposed to do, playing a role and out of bounds of normal dialogue.

The difference between trying to get the pupils to do their best and forcing them to work is a fine one. The problem for teachers is how to show concern without making it seem like a confrontation. Pupils resent being forced to do things as if every task were a kind of punishment. This is a psychological state which is easy to reach, where every piece of encouragement is interpreted as force, every cajoling as a personal attack.

> I don't like my teacher because she pushes us too hard. She is all right, but she says that if you get under a certain mark you get a detention even if you're not really brainy. She like punishes you, even if you've done your best. It makes me not want to do anything. It makes me feel I used to like it at first but now I just don't want to go anymore. I have to though. (girl, year 10)

However well-intentioned they are, and however professional, teachers are often placed in such a position that there is a possibility of a sense of confrontation, that the yearned for sharing of learning is replaced by the demands of control. This is why the sense of guessing, of trying to work out what is wanted is instructive about the system as a whole. It is as if it were based on two quite separate interpretations and understandings of the world, without mutual overlap.

> It's a bit boring when it gets going on. Teachers just go on and on and on. I just suppose they want to get it into your head, don't they? (girl, year 11)

Even when the motivation is pure, the notion of personal learning is replaced by that of 'getting it into your head', of forcing matter on reluctant victims.

The system creates the conditions in which teachers can be alienated from those they seek to help. The pupils interpret many events, from small rules to the dictates of the curriculum, as a kind of confrontation where they are supposed to follow the guidelines whether they like it or not. This is bad for the pupils and disturbing for the teachers. The pupils can take general rules personally, and instruction as a personal attack. While the teachers are carrying out policies and playing their roles, they can be disliked – not for what they stand for or the roles they play – but as if their own personalities were deeply involved in the system. Whilst most pupils learn to adapt, to accustom themselves to the conditions, there are also some who will seek out personal confrontations. This is often a matter of taking offence, even when it is not meant to be given.

> Teachers getting on your nerves, things like that. Like I said earlier, she doesn't like me and I don't like her. (boy, year 10)

In the ethos of school, such a personal conflict is not supposed to exist. The relationships are not supposed to be personal, but at a more anonymous level. Teachers are there to 'deliver', to convey, to enforce the collective rules.

> The teachers get at you for any little thing like wearing shoes to school. You have to wear shoes, if they see you with trainers on they expect you to go home and change them straight away. I don't really see the need to that. (boy, year 10)

It is the constant possibility of confrontation, and the sense of two opposite camps, that makes pupils strike their attitudes to teachers collectively. Teachers become a generalisation, the 'they' of an enemy.

The criticism of teachers needs to be understood, because is a background to all the many ways in which teachers learn to overcome the problems, or at least mitigate them. It is despite these things that teachers do a good job; by understanding the conditions rather than ignoring them. The mixed attitudes to teachers are all based on the tensions between their role as a part of the system and the occasional glimpse of the possibilities of something so much better. The question is where the two 'sides' expressed individuality position themselves.

> Now the teachers say that we should have respect to them teaching us and we should be listening to them. (girl, year 11)

At once, the idea of respect, which is often interpreted as a matter of individual rights rather than responsibilities is questioned because the teachers are insisting upon it. One cannot plead for what is supposed to be taken for granted. The distancing derives from the separation of the concept of real teaching and that of passively 'listening'.

> I don't really like that idea, because sometimes I thought the teachers don't be really nice to us and they usually boss us around and when we do ask for help they don't tend to give the help that you need. (girl, year 11)

In this interpretation, there is no two-way understanding but an assumption that there are 'bosses' around. This then is connected to the lack of personal help. Listening becomes a way of keeping quiet, responding to what they are told.

> I mean, if I go to assemblies now every day, you always hear a teacher say 'we're here to help you'. But when we go there to ask for help, they don't seem to have time for you and even though you do ask for help they only give a small amount of help. So I don't like that concept. (girl, year 11)

The basic motivation to learn comes from the pupil seeking and needing help. The mission statements of schools invariably sound amenable to individual attention and responsiveness, but the conditions are not conducive to this. From the teacher's point of view, to respond fully to every request can easy become a nightmare, impossible to choose between all the different demands. It is disappointing for the pupils. They realise that they are not at the centre of attention; the teachers have other things on their mind. The pupils then find themselves being both 'bossed' and ignored. They feel themselves to be isolated and interpret this as a deliberate intention.

> Just the way they are. They say that we are going to be the next generation. They always seem to say that to us. But when it comes down, to help us they just say, 'When you go out in this whole world you will be on your own'. That's all they say. I know it by heart. (girl, year 11)

Beneath the criticism is the yearning for conversation. The pupils want to learn, to make learning into a companionable activity. They associate learning with talking, with discussion, the exploration of ideas. They associate school, on the other hand, with specific tasks, with filling the spaces of time, with copying out facts and in receiving instruction. They also realise the talking is carefully controlled and associated with disruption, rather than learning. There is an underlying logic that concludes that learning and being at school are by no means the same thing.

Teachers find themselves at the centre of this dilemma. They want to enable pupils to learn, and yet are bound up in the large complex implacable system that demands a stringent set of rules and outcomes. The creative teacher knows what he or she can get away with, narrowing the statutory orders to the point at which they can be ignored.

The desire to learn does not ever leave pupils. Whilst at primary school they will easily say that they are at school to learn, they already realise that the underlying purpose is both more narrow and more focused. The positive outcome for teachers is that they can remind their pupils of the real purpose of education and share ideas in a way that also has an impact even on official 'learning outcomes'. Recognising the inherent contradiction, knowing the undercurrents of pressure on the pupils and the way that the system sends difficult and unattractive messages about the experience of schooling means that teachers' desire to make pupils interested can be justified. Like pupils, teachers do not need simply to submit to the system.

Even disaffected pupils recognise the importance of teachers. Those who find school most difficult will tend to mix up the role the teachers play, until they symbolise all that is hateful in authority, with their individual personality, as if every command were a personal criticism. Nevertheless, if these pupils begin to explain their antipathy – not only their disillusionment with the system but their resentment with particular teachers – they recognise what they feel they have missed. The fact that pupils regret, on leaving school, that they did not get to understand their teachers better suggests that they retain an essential insight into the potential. They know that the most inspiring moments at school were when some excitement was shared, when the teacher was personally enthusiastic and involved. They understand that what makes the teacher important is the sign of personal individual interest, a concern with the pupil and not simply the results.

The pupils' insight into the art of teaching, which combines this curious combination of role and personality, centres on one concept. The crucial expectation is that the teacher should 'explain'.

The word 'explain' carries all kinds of connotations for the pupils. It suggests a stage beyond presenting facts or delivering instructions. It involves an element of iterative dialogue, because it is impossible to explain something without knowing what is the difficulty or misunderstanding. It also suggests concerns with the pupil and with a time necessary to have a conversation.

The absence of explanation, and having to try to guess what is wanted, of feeling wrong-footed, of not knowing what is going on, is what pupils dread and resent. Whilst a large number try to remain invisible, and to work out exactly what needs to be done in order not to make themselves noticed, all pupils at one time or another feel humiliation or failure, of not being able to keep up, of being exposed. Not understanding and feeling humiliated as a result can be traumatic, but it can also become not just a personal pain, but turned into resentment, as if the fault lies not in the absence of comprehending but in the lack of explanation.

> I sometimes wish that teachers were different. They should be able to explain better. Some teachers sometimes can't explain. So you're sometimes confused. (boy, year 10)

If the pupils are frightened of not being able to keep up, or are worried about being exposed as not understanding, then their appreciation of the ability to explain is easier to understand. There might be some teachers who bring a special magic or a shared excitement to the subject or topic but what is expected of all teachers is the ability to clarify, to explain in such a way of the pupils feel that their learning matters. They resent indifference, or the seeming indifference of not making sure that they are being understood. They appreciate the professional insight, as well as the personal knowledge, that goes into explanation.

> Most of the teachers are good. They help you when you need some help. They help me to learn and they help me to understand what they are on about. I wish I could have worked a bit harder. Going out into the big world and find out things, but then I'm a bit shy. Because you will be doing something different, and you're working, not sitting at a desk, writing. (girl, year 11)

Responsiveness is the key to the concept of explaining. It makes pupils feel that they are the centre of attention and that learning involves them. This contrasts with the ethos of being taught, being forced to carry out tasks, with having to engage with the mechanisms of skills, as with literacy and numeracy hours.

The underlying problem with not being able to understand is not only the sense of humiliation or helplessness but the conclusion that they are not capable. It means that they want to give up, to assume that they are no good and that there is no point in even trying. There are some subjects that certain pupils never come to grips with, because real teaching, real explanation was lacking. Once a teacher is associated with not being able to explain his or her subject then it is almost impossible to turn around. The subject itself becomes impossible to master.

> Maths is just so difficult. I've had three teachers now. I don't understand none of them. I mean, they just sit there and they give you all these equations, and you know, you just look at them and you can't figure them out and the difficult part is all three of the teachers explain it in a different way. I mean I can't understand it. Some of the teachers, they tend to give you textbooks, make it from there. But if they told me verbally and showed it properly step-by-step I may have understood it in that way. (girl, year 11)

The individual teacher matters. Whilst it is easy for pupils to associate schools with a system, with anonymity, with crowd control and as a place which has its main function as a social centre, they never lose sight of the fact they will all have had at least some moments when they were able to appreciate what they were doing. As constantly reiterated by ex-pupils amongst the pages of The Times Educational Supplement, it is the individual teachers who matter. It is not just the unusual teachers who count, but all who move beyond the standard expectations of policy. It is not just those teachers who are inspired to find new ways of explaining things but those who demonstrate a personal interest in their pupils. Explaining is more than a performance. It is a genuine desire to understand and to help.

The lessons that stand out are never the routine ones, and nothing to do with a core curriculum. The more the pupils have heard about the government's drive to raise standards in English and maths and to push skills, the more pupils associate the central curriculum with wearisome routine. They like those subjects that are different, where they can be active and where they can talk. Any subject that is not simply dependent on sitting still and writing is preferred. It is not because these subjects are 'soft' or undemanding or that they are indulgent to pupils' whims. They are not appreciated because pupils think they can get away with things but because they are subjects that pupils associate with learning rather than being taught. The more insistence that certain tasks ought or must be carried out, the greater the tendency to resist.

Pupils crave variety and the opportunity to explore their own ideas, preferably with each other.

> If I could do it again, I'd like to do varied subjects, like at different high schools that some of my other friends go to. They do like photography and things. I find that very interesting, and drama. We don't really do anything like that here. Like in English you hardly ever get to do any drama. And when it is you don't really do it properly. (girl, year 10)

The contrast between following interesting activities and with being made to submit quietly, even sullenly, to information is constantly reiterated. The pupils' desire for engagement is with people and with activities that make sense.

At the heart of any activity is the sense of communication. To make sense, all tasks have to be shared either in their creation or their dissemination. Activities need an audience. For this reason, the demeanour of a teacher, not just his explanations, becomes important. It is not just the subject that counts but also the teacher. When pupils rate teachers, they stress the importance of the sense of humour, the ability to share a joke. Laughter is one of the closest of human bonds. The ability to find things funny changes the association of teachers with dreadful earnestness into something far more prized.

> I would change the teachers to be more polite and to listen more to help you when you really need instead of just waiting around for someone to help you.

> To be more cheerful towards you and to well…usually and mostly it's a sad face: they just walk around grumpy. They should be smiling and polite to the pupils instead of just being grumpy and horrible like they usually are. (boy, year 10)

The best moments at school obviously depend on the teachers as well as fellow pupils; they are nearly always those of social interest. Conversely, the worst of school also depends on other people and their behaviour. It is easy for pupils to find teachers to criticise, for their distance, their indifference, for their busyness and the difficulty of responding to individual needs. This is the problem of schools, the sense of an impersonal system in which no one really matters. In this way, the school system has hardly changed from the beginning.

Such an image contrasts with what teachers would like to do and with what pupils expect of them. Teachers are in a tenuous position. They would like to have personal relationships with pupils but have to maintain discipline. They would like to be appreciated, but must not want to be liked. They need to find time to talk to pupils, but find themselves faced with many other tasks. The association of teachers with authority also means that pupils rely on them to maintain order in the classroom and to judge disputes.

Whether teachers like it or not, people think that they should also be involved in all the social interactions of the school and not simply those that take place in the classroom. There are constant disputes, the sense that 'it's not fair' prevails as much in the playground as anywhere else. In this way teachers are expected to make judgements without bias. There is an incipient respect for the teacher who tries to understand what is going on, even in the face of conflicting opinions. The very fact that the teacher can be turned to for help in disputes demonstrates an important aspect of the social life of the school. Pupils do not divide their experiences into two separate halves. They know that the most important part of what they learn is social. They learn about relationships, and about personalities, about behaviour and the reasons for it. This is the real heart of schooling. The irony is that educational policy implies that it is peripheral.

In learning about social order, power and influence pupils observe each other and the teachers. The teachers' concern with politeness, good conduct and kindness matters not only in terms of finding the time to listen and explain but in terms of attempting to overcome the gap between the curriculum and the individual lives of pupils. When teachers are criticised it is not so much for the inability to explain as the indifference that suggests they cannot be bothered. The pupils hope that at least the teacher would have enough social conscience to intervene, even with bullying.

> They just start calling you names and because you're small think they can start beating you. My parents have told me to tell the teachers because it doesn't stop

them, so I do. Most of them don't. I used to go to Mr —; he didn't do anything. (boy, year 10)

The teachers who are indifferent, who remain distant and cannot be bothered are on one side of pupils' complaints. The other side is the sense that teachers have a personal grudge against individuals, usually the most difficult ones, and that they 'pick on' them deliberately.

I'm not too keen on the teacher; he always picks on people. (girl, year 10)

No pupil dislikes firmness, but they do resent it when strictness is overdone. There are certain phrases that encapsulate either too much personal interest or two little: 'they ignore you'; 'they pick on you'.

This balance between the two extremes is very important. Pupils expect teachers to have charisma. This does not mean anything exceptional. Instead, it means that there is a sense of authority that should come automatically but at the same time pupils are grateful for approachability. Without that authority, that sense of purpose, the personality is not important. Standing on dignity, however, maintaining the pomp of one's own position, is equally unsuccessful.

Pupils know instinctively who has authority. These are the ones who have integrity, who are clear about what they say and stick to it, to show a real interest in pupils without a personal desire to be liked. Pupils also know which teachers have their own real interests at heart, are comfortable with themselves and therefore curious about the well-being of all pupils.

6

Teachers as they see themselves ... and as others see them

Each teacher is, of course, an individual. This is our strength. We have to be true to ourselves. But there are certain attributes that have become like stereotypes.

The attitudes of teachers towards themselves depend on the context in which they find themselves. Many stereotypical stances have been atavistically entrenched in the public consciousness, like the comparative respect of the 'master' in a boarding school, or the assumption that to be translated from an infant to a junior school is some kind of promotion. The feelings about those who teach in nurseries, however complex this is, are different from those accorded to a secondary subject specialist. The understanding of people is not given the same status as knowledge of a discipline.

The ways in which the different types of school are viewed also vary, often according to personal experience and social attitudes. But there are also deeply held assumptions about school, a sense of suspicion and dislike, as well as ambition. There is a well-developed competition amongst some parents to gain advantage for their children by placing them in favoured schools, an attitude reflected in estate agents' commendations about location. This suggests either confidence in the effects of a school in the era of league tables, or responsibility to their offspring for the future. At all levels, schools matter, for better or worse, and therefore the teachers who are in them matter as well.

Whilst the competition for places is most developed in the leafy suburbs, there is a more widely held belief in the importance of school amongst all parents. While the government asserts that parents do not rate teachers and schools highly, most surveys demonstrate that parents approve of their children's school. There is a strong desire in the present compulsory system for schools to work, to enable the pupils to gain some kind of advantage, in terms of knowledge and awareness of conduct.

These attitudes to individual schools are, however, in the context of a deeper suspicion. If one reads novels in which schools play a part, and autobiographies where teachers are mentioned, it is negative images that abound. The sense of emotional and even physical oppression dominates. This negative attitude towards schools goes back a long way. The question remains: given that schools have not fundamentally changed over the years, have there been major shifts of attitudes towards teachers, or does the same underlying suspicion linger?

In much literature, schools are presented as forbidding, secret, meaningless and harmful, as if all the latent memories of personal experience came to the fore beneath the tendencies towards nostalgia. Schools have been viewed with antipathy; from the beginning of the state education system, to the debate whether schools for everyone was a good idea to the suspicion that they might teach all things ending in '-ion' rather than practical skills.

> Its atmosphere was oppressive and disagreeable; it was crowded, noisy and confusing; half the pupils dropped asleep, or fell into a state of waking stupefaction. The teachers, animated solely by good intentions, had no idea of execution and a lamentable jumble was the upshot of their kind endeavours.
>
> (Dickens 1865, *Our Mutual Friend*: 201)

Dickens strikes a typical note. He has a great deal of sympathy for the teachers who do their best but in a system which strikes him as mechanical and too much like a factory to be successful. There is something familiar in all this. Whilst not all writers agree that the intentions of the teachers are good, even if the execution is fallible, there is always a sense that they are working in a constricting regime, in institutions that have not been properly thought through.

One theme of the novels of the nineteenth century is the analogy of schools with factories (rather than prisons), with meaningless rote learning being forced into the production line of unwilling pupils. This means that teachers are seen as people forced to do things that are narrow and repetitive, either unwillingly or – to the writer's greater disappointment – happy in their narrow-mindedness to conform to the system. In *Middlemarch* (Eliot 1872), for example, even Mary Garth who is a natural teacher feels she does not fit the conformist mode:

> I have tried being a teacher, but I am not fit for it: my mind is too fond of wandering on its own way. (p. 166)

There is distaste fuelled by snobbery for the very idea of being a teacher: 'going from your work to teach the second form' (p. 122).

These associations with the drudgery of teaching are exemplified further by Dickens.

> He [Bradley Headstone] had acquired mechanically a great store of teacher's knowledge. He could do mental arithmetic mechanically, sing at sight mechanically, blow various wind instruments mechanically, even play the great church organ mechanically. From his early childhood up, his mind had been a place of mechanical storage.
>
> (Dickens 1865, *Our Mutual Friend*: 204)

Headstone is depicted as the perfect product of the system. 'In good time you are sure to pass a creditable examination and become one of us', he says to his protégée (p. 203). He is depicted as a typical indication of the school: the set curriculum, the lack of freedom and imagination, and the lack of any sense of personal purpose. Dickens deplores the lack of the lightness in learning and concludes that the state is imposing its mechanical will in an oppressive form: 'But all the place was pervaded by a grimly ludicrous pretence that every pupil was childish and innocent' (p. 201).

This is a system that Dickens criticises. His famous passages about schoolmasters of various appalling or terrifying types are far more slight than his depiction of the grinding monotony of meaningless teaching.

In such a system the teacher is bound to be despised, if not pitied and in this there is an element of snobbery. The schoolmasters in the state system had little status and it is easy to see most struggling in vain to win some respectability for their efforts.

> Mrs Vincy had never been at her ease with Mrs Garth and frequently spoke of her as a woman who had to work for her bread – meaning that Mrs Garth had been a teacher before her marriage.
>
> (Eliot 1872, *Middlemarch*: 264)

The ease with which characters in nineteenth-century novels could feel superior to teachers is made most apparent in the way that Eugene Wrayburn, gentlemanly, self-indulgent and expensively educated uses the term 'schoolmaster' as a term of derision.

> 'You think of me as of no more value than the dirt under your feet', said Bradley to Eugene. 'I assure you, schoolmaster', replied Eugene, 'I don't think about you.'
>
> (Dickens 1865, *Our Mutual Friend*)

Traditions of attitudes

The position of teachers in society has always been equivocal. This is not a matter of fashion or cultural attitudes but the result of the context in which they find themselves. Teachers are like social workers. They are in the anomalous position of being employed by the state, but rather than carrying the authority of the state, they see themselves as representing their clients. There was a time when, like teachers, social workers embodied all the significance of 'the man from the ministry', like the district nurse telling people what to do and having the confidence that she would be accepted. Many teachers, like various forms of social workers, look back at the time when their status was assured and when they had the sense of their place in the structures of society.

Like social workers who fight for their clients against the very people who are their employers, teachers are caught between the demands of the state in all its statutory commands and inspection, and the needs of the pupils. There have been many examples, satirised in novels, where teachers have embraced the dictates of the system and seen themselves simply as giving out instructions as they are themselves instructed. Their role is interpreted as 'deliverers' of the curriculum, as carrying out the orders that are seen as the best examples of collective enterprise. And yet, teachers also prize their autonomy and the sense that they are professionals who know what they are doing. It is an international conclusion from research that the more independence schools and teachers have, and the less interference from outside, the better they do. But this is not how it is seen by those who are in control of the system.

While the position and ethos of schools has not fundamentally changed over the years, there have been subtle shifts of emphasis and many teachers would argue that they live in a particularly difficult time. There have always been questions about whether teaching is a real profession. This is a status long and painfully sought and yet the distinction between the well-established professions like law or medicine and new ones, like teaching, remain.

Teaching as a profession

The concept of a 'profession' is complex and changing. In its original form it is based on professing a commitment to a subject, as in the idea of a professor. It implies the mastery of the subject, its defence, the protection of a body of knowledge. This is the heart of the problem. The established professions like law or medicine protect their knowledge from outsiders as keenly as their status. In this sense knowledge is power. The position of knowledge creates a small body of people who use it and only give it away for profit. Anyone entering into the field is vetted, not just for promise but for the belief in retaining this body of knowledge. And yet teachers are supposed to give away knowledge freely. They are not supposed to have arcane mysterious secrets that only they possess. They neither guard their knowledge nor rely on its possession for status.

Giving away knowledge freely goes against one atavistic tendency in professionalism. An academic, for example, must master the subject and protect it against intruders. He will not only create a specialism of his own, choosing it with care, but try to create a network of like-minded people to mark a clear territory that only they truly understand, either welcoming newcomers or telling members that they are not good enough (or, being academics, both at the same time). The sense of a profession is of one discipline that no one else truly understands. The mystery of power stems from control through the creation of a specific language that only insiders truly comprehend (or pretend they do).

This interpretation of the word 'profession' explains both the yearning for status and its protection. Of course the word can be twisted beyond recognition as in 'professional foul' which goes against any interpretation of the word other than cynicism. Nevertheless, as the analogy with social work implies, it is hard for teachers to define professionalism in terms that make sense to those who jealously guard their status. Teachers deal with giving away their secrets while doing practical things. The conditions in which they mostly work are not only utilitarian but are not of their own making, even if the pupils feel even more disenfranchised.

There have been many attempts over the years to establish teaching as a profession, including the creation of the General Teaching Council. This is apparently created as a 'Quango' to oversee self-regulation and stamp out bad practices, but the very hint that such a body could really challenge its political masters (as the judges and the Law Society can) would be quickly squashed.

There have been arguments that teachers do have a unique understanding of certain circumstances and practices, but the often-used term 'reflective practitioner' can apply to anyone who uses his or her brain to work, from building to computing as was the original definition of the term (Schoen 1987). There were also times when, as in the development of curriculum theory, attempts were made to create a body of knowledge separate from psychology and sociology, each of which was divided into different sects, only to be further subdivided (Becher and Trowler 2001). The problem is that the distinction between knowledge and practice (as still interpreted between doctors and nurses) prevails.

Teachers rightly feel that they have unique skills but that these are not fully recognised. There is little more complicated and demanding than dealing with a large cohort of individual learners. The amount of human insight and instinctive understanding is impressive. The question remains: to what extent is intelligent performance a 'body of knowledge'? Is there a well-developed theory being applied? Does it take the study of subjects or the central subject of human behaviour to demonstrate mastery? The problem for teachers in this sense is that their best practice is tacit, instinctive and immediate, not looked up first in a textbook nor properly justified by a complex language.

Those involved in teacher training (itself a telling distinction against the higher concept of education) argue the need for theory, something that helps the art of teaching to make sense. They can see the difference between the new teacher who is struggling simply to cope and the teacher who, having come through the stage of mastering the subject and the classroom, develops insights into learning behaviours of pupils that sustain their interest. Those who have the privilege to observe teachers realise how subtle and intelligent is their art, but it remains difficult to define and can never be judged by a simple checklist or by the measurement of outcomes which depend on so many other factors.

Experience and attitudes

Despite these complex abilities, some people who have been to school or have children or are a governor feel that they know about teaching in a way that they would not dream of asserting about the law or medicine. Whilst many retain a personal awareness of the status of teachers and are willing to accept their authority, they are nevertheless encouraged to assert their opinions by the government and are confident in expressing opinions as if there were not a subtle body of knowledge that gives teachers a special insight and ability to act. Parents are more ready to acknowledge teachers' prowess than politicians.

Some teachers have a problem with the way their profession is seen and interpreted. They know the complexities of their role and that there are many ambiguities in people's views of that role. The problem is that these views reveal some of the underlying dilemmas in teaching. The underlying attitudes towards teachers are fundamental and timeless (Aries 1962, Elias 1982), but these attitudes do change in subtle ways as do attitudes about any institution. It is noticeable that in the last few years there has been a determined effort by governments to change the way teachers work. Their independence and autonomy has been deliberately undermined. The Educational Reform Act (1988) created a curriculum to be enforced and controlled. Any idea of professionalism was replaced by the idea of accountability, the removal of responsibility and personal decision-making in favour of cost control and surveillance. The new managerialism, the social market of consumers and targets, has meant pressure on teachers to conform, to engage in doses of bureaucracy, to divert attention from teaching to record-keeping and assessment. Teachers are, in this jargon-ridden scenario of market forces and accountability, limited to functionaries who manage the delivery of a new curriculum system. They implement the ideas of others and they are then tested on the extent to which they have done so.

However crude the political intention, the outcomes are not that simple. The system of new managerialism is up against a far more complex reality. There might be some teachers who are willing to become functionaries and, even if the policy makers use tactics similar to the former East German police, they cannot quite enter the 'secret garden' of what takes place in the interaction of teaching and learning.

The complaints that teachers have about their conditions of work naturally centre on these new insensitive demands and on the constant harassment of inspection. Teachers feel the pressure of this interference because it goes against the natural grain of teaching. There are many books that point out that the increasingly controlling policies all over the world to change teachers and the status of teaching have been part of a gradual application of more pressure to end the mystic of teaching and to mitigate the fact that the policies do not work. Someone must accept responsibility.

The failure of such policies is always blamed on the teachers who deliver them rather than the policies themselves. Anything policy makers dictate is supposed to be (and reported as) correct; it is the fault of the teachers since good teachers cannot, let alone will not, implement the unethical and absurd. The irony is that the only way in which the education system works is because teachers mitigate its worst policies. As some research studies have discovered, the system only operates because people carry out duties they are not supposed to do. Teachers and the systems in which they operate are in constant tension.

It should be some melancholy comfort for teachers to know first that the difficulties they have are not simply a matter of the present circumstances. The ignorant, suspicious and confining policies are causing problems, but it is the historical and continuous system of schooling that will always create such problems. It is a more cheerful comfort to recognise that teachers not only go on teaching despite the policies, or indeed keep the system intact, but they do so with equanimity. It is ironic: it is the teachers' fault that the system continues since without their work the system would rightly collapse.

Who becomes a teacher

This chapter is not a polemic against the policies or against human nature that seems to inhibit people from learning, but rather about the realities of teaching. The problems are clearer and more highlighted by the exaggerated mistrust and the culture of fear (as well as spin) of the present time. If teachers are not always aware of what is going on, what about those who wish to become teachers? There are increasingly pragmatic reasons for becoming a teacher, like opportunities for power and money, which are mostly a far cry from the more traditional vocational instincts that drives people to choose to help others.

What are the reasons that people become teachers? In any endeavour there is always a mixture of motivations between the personal and professional. The fact that teaching is one of those jobs that people are aware of from the start makes a difference. Many surveys have demonstrated that the sense of personal freedom, in terms of time and autonomy, attract people for reasons that are more to do with their styles of living than the conditions of work (Day 2004, Woods 1990).

The two traditional reasons for choosing to become a teacher stem from early advice and experience, including that of parents, and the desire for economic stability. The conditions of work are important to many. These are more associated with the length of the working day or the opportunities for leave, ideas that remain more theoretical than actual. In all the mixture of motivations – and this could be true with any job – three factors stand out:

1. *Personal needs.* Personal needs is a factor that becomes more important over time. It is this, the contact with pupils, as opposed to the contractual obligations of paperwork, that strikes teachers as central, more than pay and status. The desire to help others is paramount.
2. *The value of education to society.* This is the vocational instinct, the realisation that it is possible to make a real difference and that society could be improved. It is subsumed in the differences that can be made to other people's lives, although the centre of reward has to remain theoretical. School leavers rarely thank, even if they appreciate, the efforts of their teachers. This desire to help could have unusual motivations. In several surveys of teachers giving their reasons for becoming teachers a majority included a view that they wanted to become teachers to put right their own experiences at school. They felt that they themselves had not had a pleasant time; indeed, felt even more passionate than that and wanted to spare their own pupils a similar fate. This is perhaps a mixture of satisfying a personal need with a concern for improving society.
3. *The inability to think of anything better to do.* This is of course perfectly natural. It also reinforces the idea behind the perceived status of teachers by those not involved, that 'anyone could do it'. Teachers need education but they tend to think of this as an academic qualification, as if real knowledge lay elsewhere. Other vocational tasks have years of training, like doctors, and the competition to qualify is very fierce. There is some merit to the thought that pupils can learn from anyone and that anyone, at any time in their lives, can become a teacher. Whether anyone can teach well in the present conditions is another matter.

Teaching and learning

As in any employment, a fact often underrated, personality and the integrity of the individual is paramount, and yet the role should not depend entirely on personality. There will always be tensions between different elements that make up the distinctions between teaching and learning. The two go together but they are rarely in equilibrium. The controlling policies insist almost entirely on teaching as if the children were mere ciphers. Extremes of instrumental demands are inevitably undermined but in a way that if the policies fail it is the teachers, not the policymakers, who are blamed as if the manipulators had a role like Homeric gods, interfering with human endeavour for their own sport.

At the other extreme is the natural cynicism of memory. In many autobiographical and semi-autobiographical accounts of childhood, learning is the urge of personal desire carried out despite many impediments as, for example, in H.G. Wells' *History of Mr Polly*. Nevertheless, all accounts of learning include the individual teacher who helped and who encouraged. One reason for this is that pupils have a strong desire to please the teacher. It is one of the main motivations for learning and should be used in a delicate way. But it is imperative that teachers notice the desire to please and that they detect any sign of progress so that the motivation to please is rewarded. This is the opposite of insistence or confrontation. It draws attention to the natural part of a teacher. All learning is personal but it is also social and badly needs an audience. The higher skills are a matter of communicating to appreciative people. Without such encouragement, they wither away.

The teacher is therefore not so much a manipulator as a receiver of learning. Part of the ability to explain is the ability to respond. The teacher is not supposed to know everything but to be aware of how and where to find answers, to share in the pursuit of knowledge. The teacher who is respected is not simply the one who has most force of personality but the one who indicates his own excitement in an understanding of learning.

The teacher is dedicated to learning so there is something selfless about it. All teachers say that the greatest pleasure lies in the pupils and interactions with them. This does not gain easy rewards and even makes the teacher vulnerable to those who wish to exercise control. There are many impediments to the art of enabling pupils to develop. Most of these come from outside but learning can also be undermined from within the teacher. It is partly because we have to learn to resolve the tensions between the private and public, between the role and personality, and between the personal commitment to pupils and the enforced responses to inspectors and bureaucrats.

Teachers observed

The kind of psychological pressures that undermine teachers from within come in different layers of consciousness. There is the sense of wanting to be on one's own in a private space without being overlooked, blamed, manipulated or inspected. The stress of the control of a whole class leads to the natural desire to be left in a 'secret garden' of one's own. Being a teacher should come about by being turned to, consulted and appreciated. This is not the same as being a teacher who sees him- or herself as the performer. The idea of being watched is difficult, as if we were easily undermined by criticism.

Teachers, like pupils, suffer from a desire to please. If they cannot force pupils to be obedient or responsive, they still want to be appreciated; most of all by the very people who are observing them. It is important to overcome this version of self-consciousness, to have the integrity to act without the hidden desire for praise.

This desire to please is partly a result of all the external controls and constraints, the feeling of being watched and judged, not only in the performance but by the outcomes. Teachers have a tendency to be too self-deprecating. We are often swayed to do things against our better judgement by those in power. We are not only told constantly what to do but actually do it. This leads not to praise or understanding but the opposite. Teachers are not appreciated and not respected for their willingness to do what is asked of them. The willingness to give, even to the point of self-sacrifice, which is the great virtue of teachers, is also the reason that they are so vulnerable to external criticism.

Teachers need to understand the particular culture they find themselves in so they are not so vulnerable to its abuses. In all the analyses of the present time there are certain characteristics that all people will recognise. At the core is a realisation that teachers are useful and giving, which runs counter to the philosophy of selfish individualism. That there is 'no such thing as society' but only individuals thinking about themselves and competing selfishly for themselves undermines the whole idea of teaching. To this individualism of market forces glistening with the gloss of spin, is added the assumption that it is 'not what you do but how you sell yourself' that counts. The pupils are aware of this culture. This is demonstrated not just theoretically in government policy, but in its manifestation in the practices of inspection.

The trouble for teachers is that the implications of accountability are pervasive. Accountability means that you have to watch your back, to be fearful of anything that might be construed as giving offence. It is better to do nothing than to get it wrong. Accountability is the opposite of responsibility. It means a lack of trust, and implies that teachers need to be inspected as they must have a tendency to do wrong. Everything must be accounted for in writing as if what is not written up is deemed never to have taken place. This controlling tendency leads to a culture of fear. If a teacher so much as touches a child there is the threat of litigation. There is a readiness to take offence at every action.

Conclusions

The underlying conclusion is that teachers cannot be trusted and this leads to the pupils' ambivalent views of them. They have been brought up in the culture of individualism and personal rights and to be suspicious of others and their motivations. There are many ironic undercurrents in such a pervasive attitude, like the desire to look for offence, like the weight placed on any misuse of language, however innocently deployed, since it is something that can be detected and proved.

It is the equivalent of 'being in writing'. This can lead to the assumption that all men are potential offenders and assumed guilty until cleared by the Criminal Records Bureau. The culture of suspicion has become enshrined in large if ineffective institutions which are designed to attack the potential wrongdoings of taxpayers, fathers, single mothers and others, including teachers.

Teachers' reactions to scrutiny

The teacher needs to be aware of the symptoms of this cultural ethos not just because he or she has to be careful, like avoiding school outings, however highly beneficial they may be, but because they have the potential to undermine any real education and because they can undermine individual teachers. By restricting teachers' authority and by keeping them constantly under suspicion, it is too easy for teachers to see themselves as victims. The important matter is to have the courage of our convictions so that whilst institutions and instrumental policies are deeply flawed, the integrity of our own position is kept up.

Governments use both sticks and carrots to demonstrate their command. The carrots are particular rewards to those who comply most readily, whether in schools like 'beacon schools' or 'academies' or 'specialist centres' or individuals like 'advanced teachers'. The sticks are more pervasive and more rhetorical. Whilst they are made clear in the inspectorial regimes, they are surrounded by the command structures of raising standards, setting targets, introducing new initiatives and constantly attacking failed schemes and failing schools. The rewards are for conformity but they are ephemeral compared to the fear of exposure.

The result of this is can be that teachers feel vilified or marginalised. Their attitudes to their own profession illustrate the same feelings. Teachers are aware of the poor image of their profession and of the constant 'teacher bashing'. There was once a cartoon of two teachers in a staff room. One says to the other, 'The Secretary of State says he cares for and cherishes teachers … What would it be like if he didn't?' The sense of low status and little recognition is exacerbated by the pace and nature of change and the constant increase in workloads and expectations. The central problem for teachers is the sense that they are controlled and this goes against the whole spirit of teaching, which is essentially a voluntary response to other people's desire to learn. The command structures of instruction, like set tasks and tests, is against both the spirit of learning and teaching so that the flaw in the educational system goes deep. The irony is that there is also pressure on teachers not just to submit but to employ their own kind of spin, to prove that they are doing things. The time spent demonstrating that they are carrying out requirements takes away the time from doing their job. Much of their time is spent doing bureaucratic procedures which puts pressure on them and means that they have to make sure that their pupils are also occupied in the same way. Hence the stress on all the writing and on the tests. This is all part of the culture of surveillance, of manufacturing consent to keep teachers so occupied that they have no time to object. Besides, speaking out against the regime is also attacked; any dissent is made an illegitimate.

It is sometimes surprising how teachers, head teachers, advisers and others have put up with this attack on their autonomy and on their very jobs. The universities have also been weakened and the powerful body of vice-chancellors has submitted to the worst interests of their own institutions. This, however, is the secret of the policy-makers' success. They not only have financial muscle but know how to divide and rule. By the use of competition, by selective rewards and individualised punishment, there is little collective or co-ordinated protest. Those who complain feel isolated.

Teachers find themselves in a difficult position because they are dedicated to nurturing their pupils, and instead of feeling anger that this task is made more difficult, they feel guilt. They rest on the ethics of care but no one seems to care about them. In this they are like their pupils. They have no voice so they both understand the implications of what is happening but feel their complaints should be kept private. As in the case of pupils, constant silencing renders them inarticulate.

The culture of competitive individualism and the decay of traditional values and roles divides pupils from their teachers and both feel the strain. The whole point of education is the unity of the endeavour. Pupils and teachers are essentially on the same side but at the core this joint enterprise has been undermined. 'Divide and rule' depends on teachers being essentially separated from their pupils as well as from their parents. Any educational system like the one in operation over many years will have this flaw but it is one exacerbated at the present time. This should make the essential fault line more apparent, if only people had time to see it. The problem for teachers goes deeper. The institutionalising of their roles, against their own pupils, causes such fundamental disquiet that much of a teacher's time is spent mitigating this fact.

The institutionalising of blame, in setting up agencies of control heightens what has long been a concern. The collective memories of many individuals about the educational experience, their sense of displacement, disappointment and even trauma brings to the surface long-held concerns. As civil servants used to be fond of saying, 'every regulation has the opposite effect to that intended'. Whilst the law against abuse gets more stringent, cases of abuse multiply. Those who make the laws are not always aware of their consequences.

The cultural policies that are mentioned here help to clarify why teachers find themselves in an ambiguous position. They complain about workloads and deplore all the time they must spend ignoring their essential tasks but they should also see that matters could be different.

In the systems of education that are employed all over the world there are, despite the differences, some shared dilemmas about teachers' roles (Alexander 2000). In institutional organisations teachers have to be aware of playing a number of different and sometimes contradictory roles. While some governments stress just one role and focus on one aspect, teachers are conscious of several. Teaching can be seen as the transmission of information and skills. This can depend on knowledge of the subject or on the mechanisms of administration. This is what can be easily measured.

- Teaching can also be an induction into a culture, a way of thinking, attitudes and assumptions. This suggests that the kind of knowledge being conveyed is of a far more subtle type.
- Part of what teaching demonstrates is the value as well as the culture of the society. By the way the teacher behaves, he or she shows the powers of shared reflection and respect for others through the rules of good conduct.
- The teacher is also a facilitator who recognises the needs and aspirations of the young and enables them to find self-belief. This book argues that this role cannot be separated from the others and is no simple matter of emotional nurturing.
- The teacher is also an accelerator, the scaffold on which the individuals build on their own aspirations and endeavours. This includes the stringency of high expectations and demands.
- And teachers are people with individual abilities, who craft a complex art and who understand learning and its enablement until it seems instinctive. This is the 'theory' of teaching that makes it special, something which is rarely recognised except by the individuals who benefit and who take it for granted since such prowess is based on not drawing attention to itself.

The art of teaching is subtle because it is individual and it rests on the recognition of the power and importance of learning rather than that of instruction, a much easier matter. It is complex because learning consists not just of the academic acquisition of knowledge but social and cultural awareness of personal and emotional fulfilment (Egan 1997). The blending of the different strands and balances of rights and responsibilities make teaching into a subtle responsive but authoritative art. There is always a balance to be struck between responsibility and accountability, between leadership and managerialism, between real effectiveness and proved efficiency, between influence and compliance, and between education and training.

7

Teachers' relationships with parents
A tragedy of errors

Parents should be the natural allies of teachers, and yet a whole history of research reveals a series of troubled relationships and ambiguous roles. This has come about partly because teachers have neglected parents, or remained aloof from them. Teachers are busy with what they are doing, so they tend to resent any outside interference, however natural or proper it might be. They are further bolstered by a tradition that is rooted in private education in which the role of the schoolmaster is paramount. Those schools, which depend on parents as paying clients, are those in which the teachers most completely hold their authority as sacrosanct.

The lack of close relationships between parents and teachers, despite many attempts to overcome it, is a tragedy. This is for two reasons. The first is that the power of the position and of being *in loco parentis*, should remain in the hands of the most willing of teachers, yet has been usurped by the state. By not forging close relationships with parents, and by not fostering them and their interests as a source of support, the teaching profession has allowed politicians to dictate not only conditions of service but the curriculum and teaching styles. The interests of parents are not the same as those of politicians, but their silence has allowed the imposition of inspections, examination and testing policies and an emphasis on the instrumental as well as on measurement and competition that parents do not actually approve of, any more than teachers do.

The second reason for the tragedy of absence of a close relationship between parents and teachers is that schools have become the playthings of government because their roots are so shallow. The emphasis on schools as hermetically sealed units, cut off from the social and economic realities of the communities and families from which the pupils come, means that their real power for change is very limited. Whilst it might suit some teachers with a particular cast of mind to think of their role as purely academic, presenting their subjects like personal fiefdoms of interest, such academic exclusiveness neglects most of the educational realities. There is no social research that does not acknowledge the crucial influence of the home and the neighbourhood. This fact might be the despair of the policy makers but it has to be acknowledged. By the time that pupils enter school much of their education – attitudes, motivations, understandings, world view – is already firming up. This means that teachers are sidelined. They are not so much educators as trainers. Whilst most everyone has the memory and experience of a great teacher, this is not applicable to the education system as a whole, and it is this distinction between the whole person and the role of an education system that will be pursued in this chapter.

Ambiguities abound, but amidst these complexities is one fundamental reason why teachers are so beleaguered, so exposed, so manipulated and so marginal. Parents could and should be close allies. They could prevent the hysteria of policy making and the downgrading of professionalism. They could help define the larger and more profound social role of teachers. And yet, the tragedy is that this natural alliance has never been at the heart of education policy.

Parents play a crucial, if mostly marginal, role in the lives of teachers. They provide the raison d'être for schools, providing the already-formed pupils. It is an interesting insight into the way teachers are led to think that even this provision of a pupil can be resented. There are many case studies on teaching reading, for example, where the parents are asked not to interfere with their children's decoding of text, because they might be doing it wrong, as if teacher methodology were more important than the pleasures of personal interaction. Some parents, exasperated by this infringement of their pleasure in stories and in reading to their child wondered whether some teachers wished them not to enable their children to use language at all, in case that was not done according to a correct method.

Whilst parents are crucial, their role becomes increasingly marginalised as their children grow older. And yet their influence on pupil attitude and expectation remains powerful. Beneath the great demarcation line between home and school, one fostered by the pupils themselves, lie the subtle attitudes towards schooling and the future, towards the daily experience of school and the good it is supposed to do. Parents have their memories, as we will see, and these inform the mindset of their children. Teachers are, of course, aware of this and pass on labels about particular families, or impressions about the backgrounds of difficult pupils. At the same time parents are not necessarily seen as allies when it comes to difficulties; they are depicted as part of the problem. To this extent teachers acknowledge the significance of the home background but they tend to do so negatively, with suspicion and blame, rather than in the spirit of co-operation.

Parents have an interest in their children's schools, but do not have much choice of school in the public sector. This power of choice is invoked by governments as an instrument of ultimate sanction, as if teachers ought to be continually aware of the feelings of their clients. Governments invoke parents as the people for whom they act. Their policies are assumed to be in accordance with parents' wishes, even if they are not and parents are pitted against the very schools with which, through their children, they are connected. Parents are also used deliberately as controlling agents, sitting on governing boards, attending annual meetings at which governors are held accountable. In recent years parents, through successive changes to the role of governing boards, have been offered the possibility of managerial control.

On the other hand, parents are also put into the role of supporters, friends and helpers. Through parent-teacher associations, out-of-school clubs, or as additional unpaid staff, they have found themselves willingly made into colleagues and collaborators, serving the needs of teachers rather than controlling them. Parents fulfil a number of roles, from ancillary helpers to governors, from representatives of individual pupils to the ostensible excuses for policy, from choosers of schools and readers of league tables, to supporters as well as critics.

At the heart of these diverse and ambiguous roles are some fundamental dilemmas. One is the tension between the two opposing views of parents; are they acting as partner or as police officer? Are they essentially helpers and supporters, forming their children's attitudes and expectations, attending school functions, aiding teachers and helping to raise money? Or are they essentially the ultimate sanction, the people who have an inspectorial role on policy, on appointments, and all the other matters still in the hands of governors? There are many examples of both.

An even more profound question is that of responsibility. Where does true moral authority lie: in the home or in the school? Are teachers there purely to present a curriculum, or are they social workers, teaching good behaviour as well as knowledge? This dilemma is shown up in the contrasting attitudes to teachers in France and in England. In France the social responsibility is agreed to lie firmly in the hands of parents. The teachers have quite a different function. In Great Britain, particularly in primary schools, the parents see teachers as responsible for moulding their children's behaviour.

This ambiguity about the role of the teacher is shared by the teachers themselves. Those committed to their subjects, particularly in secondary schools, will assert their rights to be free of all social responsibility and pass that firmly back to parents, to social workers and to other teachers. Many teachers, will, however, be drawn into the complexities of emotional and social problems, whether they like it or not. Indeed, it is the very prevalence of these problems that cause many of them to be suspicious of parents.

Parents view teachers as falling somewhere between the two extremes of complete aloofness and friendly approachability, between the role of authoritarian and autonomous experts, and as collaborative and sympathetic partners. In either case, parents take a real interest in the role of teachers and their effects on their children. Despite this personal curiosity and empathy, parents are invoked by policy makers as the real supporters of government policy. When governments proclaim that they are *in loco parentis*, like at a boarding school, they make two assumptions. They assume that their policies are supported, even if the teachers do not like them and they assume that they can declare a view on behalf of teachers. Both assumptions are mistaken. Parents view government policies with mixed feelings of suspicion and helplessness, and their attitudes towards teachers are far more trusting and sympathetic.

It is partly because of parents' feelings for teachers as individuals that they view present policies in many countries with some alarm. This is not a matter which is well advertised, nor one that teachers have seized on. Indeed, suspicion of government policies would undermine their legitimacy, not only because there is a call for adaptability, individualism and skills to compete on the international market, but because this is what parents are supposed to want. In two research studies it was established that parents did not see themselves on the same terms that the larger political world saw them. They did not like their being described as 'consumers' – they saw the point of such a term but felt their interests and needs to be incompatible with such motivations, including criticism and power. The reason for this was their attachment to the teachers they knew and the school with which they were familiar. The government in question dismissed these research findings on the spurious grounds that parents are sentimental about the particular schools that their own children attend but are still on the side of government policies and other agencies involved in inspections (Cullingford 1996).

A second piece of research was carried out specifically to explore parents' attitudes towards the main points of government policy. The policies were most strongly commended by government, resented by teachers and questioned by parents. Partly to separate parents from teachers and partly to use them as a means of putting more pressure on teachers, the policy, duplicated in principle in various parts of the world, was outlined in a propaganda leaflet called the 'Parents' Charter'. The fact is that parents and teachers were equally alarmed at the principles but there was no public dialogue about it. The teachers went on suffering silently and the parents inarticulately.

The major thrust of this policy is the relationship between buyer and seller, with the market controlled by inspection. On the banner headlines presented to them the parents voiced either suspicion or anger. They were told that a new reporting system could clarify exactly how their children were performing, yet they we suspicious of it. They were presented with the idea of the clarity and efficiency of test results at 'key stages' but found them unhelpful and obscure. They found performance tables, supposed to be a source of curiosity and delight, meaningless and unbelievable. They denied having any real choice (unless they were rich). They derided the National Curriculum and felt that it was neither broad nor balanced. They mistrusted the reports from inspectors and avoided going to the public meetings of governors when the schools were supposed to give an account of themselves. Indeed, the parents in both surveys were suspicious of the policies, not on the grounds of party loyalty but because once they had the effects outlined, once they had to address them, they found they clashed with their own beliefs and experience.

Here should have been a real opportunity of a major alliance between teachers and parents. The findings are clear, if unreported: the common agreement is manifest but ignored. The problem is that the lack of a common voice between teachers and parents is based on a lack of dialogue, to the damage of both but more significantly for the teachers. There is ambiguity about the role of parents that comes about because of their comparatively temporary involvement. The power parents are supposed to have, as governors and clients, rarely impinges on the lives of teachers. Teachers continue unaffected by the world outside the routines of school, to their cost. The real problem is not only lack of communication but of the differences of outlook. It is not that parents inhabit different worlds but they have very different frames of thought and approach. It is teachers who give the impression of living in a world of their own, legitimate but unconnected to the language of parents.

One could argue that the separation of parents' interests, with their broad sense of education, their emotional intuitions and their individual interests, will always be distinct from the machinery of public testing. It could be suggested that successive governments find it convenient to be uncontaminated with the awkward questions of the wider social sphere. How much easier it is to control a system that can be measured, which has targets and outcomes, clear goals and results. But it could also be possible that this lurch towards an independently defined and complete system has been a move in the wrong direction, a loss of the sense of the whole individual replaced by the interests of the organisation, where the clearer the relationship between intended strategy and measured outcome the better.

There is always a strong appeal about a complete institution, self-contained like a ship, as autonomous as an island. There is the sense of collective understanding defined against an outside body or the outside world which helps to bolster the standing of members of the organisation with each other. Teachers are doubly embroiled in the legitimacy of institutions with their own school and with the schooling system as a whole. Any intruder in a complete system, even a client for a product, very easily becomes a slight threat, someone upsetting or unsettling. And yet parents are known to be supporters of schools, extending their hopes and believing in the efficacy of what could be achieved for their offspring.

Given the institutional nature of schools it is not surprising that they have found it difficult to accommodate even the most well-meant offers of parents. There have been times when the role of parents as potential helpers in a school has not only been recognised but invoked. There have been many occasions in which parents, particularly at infant and primary school levels, have been welcomed into the school, encouraged to participate and cajoled into assisting the teacher. The old notices 'no parent beyond this point' were removed and attempts made to find them distinct and useful tasks. The initiatives were many and widespread. And yet, despite the good intentions, most of them were deemed to be unsuccessful. The parents, being emotionally allowed onto the inner sanctuary, were unsure what was expected of them. With teachers embarrassed by the presence of others, particularly with those who might have educational prowess or qualifications, the presence of outsiders became a matter of control, with the teacher remaining central. Helping in the classroom became a matter of carrying out routine tasks. There were misunderstandings and tensions. Even those parents who should have had a particular interest in their child's unique disability found themselves in conflict with teachers. The fundamental principle of teacher role and hegemony remained unchanged.

Despite all the attempts to involve parents in the classroom, problems were unresolved. The suspicion of other people's presence in the classroom kept being expressed. The problem was that parents were not seen as having a legitimate interest in their children, but instead as a professional intrusion. They were given menial tasks and never invited to teach. They were prevented from any meaningful intervention. Indeed the most vociferous objections were raised about the 'mother who thought she was a teacher'. The teachers felt threatened by the presence of strangers and jealous of their professional role.

At one level this seems obvious. But at another it is somewhat odd, as if we had invented a role for its own sake. Here are adults concerned with the education of individuals and wanting to foster the development and the learning of all. And yet, the education of the young or, more pointedly, the initiation into skills and the demands of exams are taken over by specialists trained in the delivery of the state's requirements. The classroom is sacrosanct and parents entering in are rendered anonymous and intrusive. At best no one is certain about what the parent is supposed to be doing. The teacher remains in natural command and is challenged to find routine ancillary tasks to keep the outsider occupied.

All this says a lot about the status of the teacher in the classroom and the completeness of the enclosure it represents. The teacher has always been accepted as in complete command of her or his small kingdom. This is still accepted by parents who have themselves experienced the autonomous command of teachers. There is a widespread assumption that the teacher knows what is going on, has to direct and control it and is creating the best, most recognisable conditions in which pupils learn. Parents do not wish to intrude into this domain. As the studies of teachers in the classroom demonstrate, there is shyness as well as ambiguity about their role. They know the teacher remains in command, and that parents have no more authority than an ancillary worker, despite their interest in their own children.

Parents are traditionally loathe to intrude into the classroom, whatever their personal interest. The government, on the contrary, has deliberately and persistently encroached on this 'secret garden', on the autonomy and authority of the teacher in the classroom. Where parents fear to tread, the government policies have not only dictated the curriculum but have measured out the times and even the styles of teaching. There has been a big shift of emphasis from the role of the teacher, with professional autonomy, respected and trusted, to the new understanding of the teacher as a functionary, told what to do, what targets to achieve, and measured accordingly. Within this new regime, the parents, whilst invoked as the ultimate clients, and the most demanding ones, indeed as the real raison d'être of government policy, find themselves sidelined. Added to the traditional separateness of the teacher in the classroom is the added enclosure of government policies. Parents are excluded not just by tradition but by the very policies set up in their name.

Parents nevertheless come into contact with teachers on a daily basis, from the delivery of their children to their picking them up. The issue of parental rights as governors, or as attending the annual formal meetings is a quite separate one. Parents do have to approach a school and teachers, even if they do not encroach too far. They receive reports and can attend parents' evenings to hear about the progress of the child as well as the development of new policies. The relationship evoked here is still a formal one. Parents have rights and the teachers are told they are accountable to them. The irony is that the more formal the relationship between parents and teachers, the less the parents believe in them and the less they learn from them. If one takes report writing as an example, it is clear that there has been a change of style and tone from the kinds of reports that used to be produced annually and the carefully measured ones that now have to be produced by law, stipulating exactly what the child has achieved against the key stages, the targets and the national averages. Teachers must conform to the demands of report writing. The result is that parents no longer trust the reports or find them useful. The more standard the language, the more measured the description of the targets that have been achieved, the less helpful parents find the reports. Formality and accountability is not what they are after. All the information about standard assessment tests seem to them meaningless. Parents still want a more personal, more individual and penetrating insight into the performance of their children.

The real relationships of parents and teachers remain far less formal. They can take place at any time, and, in theory at least, are cherished by parents. The amount of time parents come into contact with teachers, at least in primary school is considerable – about half an hour per week. The potential for traditional personal relationships is there. The fact is, however, that these contacts are not so much to do with academic progress or personal needs but with routine problems of illness or absence. It could be argued that the place for more formal, academic discussion is not the occasional evenings set aside for accounting for what has been done. But parents long for more immediate informal discussions. Because of the time constraints many of these informal contacts are negative, dealing with routine matters that have gone wrong. For busy teachers parents are loyal supporters and potentially useful aids. In practical terms, however, parents can be a problem. They take up time. They are an additional burden. As one teacher typically pointed out:

> While these meeting contacts with parents are very important I feel they are an additional strain on the workload.

Parents are not presented with regular opportunities to meet with teachers; five minutes per child per year is the official time in many school consultative evenings. Contacts about the individual needs of children could be useful to teachers but they find themselves spending time with parents discussing more pressing, more routine matters. Teachers find themselves reacting to parental pressure, rather than using parents in a consultative way. Part of this is due to the hegemony of the classroom, but part of it is due to the time management systems of school, or lack of them. Those parents who see most of teachers tend to be the most difficult.

The relationships between teachers and parents remain troubled and confused at times, despite the mutual interest. There are many cases of aloofness, and many cases of social and fundraising harmony, as well as examples of parents as partners or police. Yet the school remains a formal institution and what happens in a school is still a private matter. Parents have no rights to intrude. They also retain a kind of trust in the professionalism of teachers. At times, the parents' sense of teachers' formality and the separateness of schools can turn into difficulty. There has always been a tradition or respect for teachers all over Europe that sees them as representative of society as a whole, whether as the embodiment of the state or as privately autonomous professionals. This latent awe of teachers is especially marked in those with less self-esteem. In areas of privation, for example, we see the insecurities or parents expressed not only in self-doubt but in a pronounced guardedness of teachers with all their official authority.

If teachers are aware of some parents in particular these will tend to be those of the more difficult pupils. When it comes to truancy or misbehaviour, parents find themselves locked in a battle with all kinds of authority, culminating in the teachers. For the excluded pupils, parents are in a difficult position. The teachers are aware of the strong influence that parents are supposed to have and will have made many judgements about home backgrounds, siblings and the parents. The sense of parents as a nuisance can culminate in a complete breakdown of relationships, in the symbolic barrier of the difference between the interests of the school and the interests of the pupil. Ultimately the teacher's first duty is to the school as a whole, for its smooth running, for minimum disruption and for the interests of the collective. No individual problem can upset all of this. Parents acknowledge this and can become overawed by the official autonomy of the system.

As the most extreme examples we can cite cases where it is not only the pupil who feels the humiliation of failure but where the parents turn away in bewilderment or anger. The parent continually brought in to be confronted by his or her child's misdemeanours is in a difficult position. Such parents are not only treated as responsible for problems but for bringing problems with them. Parents do not know how to deal with the etiquettes of discipline.

> They didn't want me to go to that school. Me mum went to see the headmaster, but me mum didn't know sort of what to do, know what I mean? She was sort of confused but she says if it keeps on our [child is] not coming to this school again. (girl, age 11)

Once parents are associated with the troubles of their children it is very difficult to create fruitful relationships. The sense of confusion and helplessness grows and parents also feel ostracised.

> Me dad even phoned up to see if I could come back, they says 'We don't want you back' and slammed the phone down. Then they didn't even bother trying. (boy, age 12)

There are many examples of the process of pupils being excluded from the system and parents are then deeply involved. These are the parents who not only suffer from a lack of confidence or even from an awe of the school, but who are treated with disrespect themselves.

> My mum explained it and said, 'Well, as long as they tell me the truth I'll go up to school.' And, like, when she did go up the teacher slammed his hand on table and treated her like a kid, so she stood up and give him a mouthful, started accusing him of this, that and the other and I never went back to school then. (boy, age 11)

These are extreme cases but they illustrate some of the difficulties of parents at the margin, and the tendency for teachers to be most aware of parents when they or their child are troublesome.

Most relationships, of course, are not so fraught. There is a genuine respect for teachers, and a mutual warmth of feeling despite some of the impediments of time, control and responsibility. Nevertheless the memories that parents have of their own schooling also influences their present attitudes towards teachers. They were also pupils once and remember the artificial awe for the role of teachers and their own place in the hierarchy of school. In their turn they have looked up to teachers, studied them, known which ones they liked or disliked and which ones they despised or feared. They too have had the experience of waiting outside the head teacher's office and been told off or punished for misdemeanours. Some of this experience remains within the atavistic consciousness of parents and can influence the way they approach teachers. When parents talk about their own experiences of school certain themes recur, like the unusual lesson that is contrary to what is supposed to be taught or the trip taken at the spur of the moment. One of these themes are the traumatic moments with some teachers.

> I just couldn't stand maths and this particular day she was giving us all these lessons. I thought she was the type of person that wouldn't sit and talk to you. She was not a very popular teacher. Anyway, she dragged me out in front of the class and she really dragged me over the coals. She really slated me for, it might have been only a couple of minutes but seems like two or three hours and I think from that day on I've had a mental block. (girl, age 12)

Whilst parents remember the general routines, the rote learning or the chanting of tables, they recall certain moments that stand out. These instances of humiliation highlight the feeling of the power that is held by teachers. What a mathematics teacher says in one lesson is seared in the memory. Only a teacher could have such a frightening effect. The parents generally recall the old days of fierce discipline, sometimes in contrast with what they perceive are the freer, easier codes of behaviour today.

> When I was at school it was much more, you were much more frightened of the teachers for a start. They were much more dictatorial and less friendly. (mother)

It is somewhat of a relief to realise that relationships with teachers do not have to be dominated by fear and respect, but some of the awe remains. Some of the atmosphere of schools and the status of teachers becomes deeply ingrained.

> The teachers had more of a disciplinary role at school. The threat was there, and what the teacher said went. If you done something wrong you would be disciplined, which made you more wary to do it. (mother)

The sense of threat and the wariness are very easily conjured up again. Schools are territories that belong to teachers. Parents witness the reactions of the pupils and are reminded of their own.

Whilst one of the deep memories of schooling is the discipline of teachers, there is also a sense of contrast between the strictness of the past and the comparative leniency of the present. Not all parents approve what they perceive as the friendlier, more relaxed atmosphere.

The teacher clouted me, whereas today things have so changed that if a child is clouted by a teacher the parent immediately goes up to the school and rants and raves and says what on earth do you think you are doing? A good clop round the ear would do some of these children a lot of good. (father)

Parents as well as teachers recognise the difficult parent and the diminishing freedom and authority of teachers who would no longer even dare to hint at retribution. Parents are all aware of the change in the status of teachers and contrast the past with the present.

This contrast of their own experience of school and what they see teachers undergoing at the present time gives parents a lot of sympathy for teachers. We have noted how they observe the official harassment of teachers, the intrusion of inspectors and the naming and shaming of individuals and schools, just as they witness the stress and the burdens of paperwork. There are a number of areas in which parental sympathy is underlined by the contrast between their own memories and what they see now. Parents give a well-rounded picture of the role of teachers, and the particular demands they are dealing with. The contrasts with the past include lower standards.

When it comes to the educational side, I think definitely it is lower standards, discipline wise, manners wise, system wise. In our days you respected your teachers, and your school. It was a discipline, like going to church or mosque. From teacher's side they are not motivated and there is not any or hardly any you will find a role model for the children. (mother)

If a teacher said something at school you took notice of what they said but now it doesn't seem to be because the parents and the education system don't allow them to. The standards are lower now. (father)

The distinction needs to be made between the idea of lower standards in the education system as a whole and lower standards of individual teachers. The loss of a sense of discipline is due partly to the changing general social mores. The lack of respect derives partly from a feeling that personal motivation has been lost and partly because the system undermines the teachers, as well as the parents. Parents might be tempted to say that 'standards', like 'discipline', are not as they used to be but their point of view is more subtle. Their sense of loss is matched by a genuine appreciation that the lighter imposition of discipline is mitigated by more human qualities of openness and friendliness.

Teaching styles seem to be much more attractive now and much more social than they used to be. (father)

It is very often more informal and that. They do consider what the children are thinking and allow them to work in groups. So I think that broader approach and understanding of what activity is instead of having to just learn by rote on your own. That must be an improvement. (mother)

Given the propensity to sentimentalise the past, and given the temptation to decry the lack of discipline in the present, it is interesting to note the equivocation of parents towards teachers in their youth as compared to the present. Teachers might appear to be more informal but they still rely on rote learning. They might lack motivation but this may be due to their working conditions. What emerges from the parents' testimony is their perception that teachers are under pressure. Teachers are doing their best in difficult circumstances.

I certainly think that there's a lot more pressure on the children now than what there was in my day and this is also an aspect of things that have changed. (father)

It's brought a lot more stress and strain upon the teachers. That's all very well for the powers that be in their ivory towers to say, 'you will do this' but for various reasons the school might not be able to reach those standards. (father)

Teachers and children are suffering from pressure. It appears that there are many more external demands, resulting in the loss of projects and going out 'into the field'. Parents talk about the way in which their own children do not receive the individual attention they hope for. The sense of strain is paramount; a loss of real autonomy and control.

I can remember that if I had a problem in the lesson, say if we had some homework and I didn't get a good mark, I remember the teacher actually keeping me behind. I think the child is too afraid to approach the teacher and when they do the teacher does not give them much help because they are rushed off their feet. (mother)

The problems for teachers are not depicted as being of their own making. Parents would prefer to see greater discipline – which means greater authority for teachers – but they would also want to observe greater freedom with less external control. Parents also have a very firm explanation for the stress of teachers, for their being 'rushed off their feet'. Teachers are suffering from the demands of the political agenda in the guise of the National Curriculum.

It can have an adverse effect on some children...it's brought a discipline into schools where teachers have got to...conform to the programme, which takes the individuality out of a teacher. (father)

Parents have mixed feelings about the National Curriculum, having heard so many arguments for it. They have constantly been told that such a regime can ensure that all subjects are taught, the minimum standards are set, and that there are no longer the possibilities of distinct weaknesses or gaps of knowledge. And yet, despite this propaganda and the plausible intentions, they miss the sense of individuality, of personal scope of the kind they remember.

> In some way it now limits…I think they are so busy trying to sort of abide by what's laid down in the National Curriculum that some areas have to go by the by, which is a shame. (mother)

This perception of teachers' constant busyness is linked to the feeling that teachers do not have time to listen, either to them or the children. The power of the centralised curriculum is such that not only are teachers' lives more closely controlled but their relationships with parents, on an informal basis which is so prized, is diminished. Schools are made that much more separate from the community when teachers' time is so dictated. If teachers do not have time for children they have even less for parents.

> They are rushed off their feet. They have to cover so much regarding the National Curriculum that the child is lagging behind…every time the parent goes back saying well, my child is not doing well, they say how do you know about it, they say they haven't got time … so many things to cover. They are covering so much that they're paying less attention to the most important subjects. (mother)

Despite the sympathy for individuals, parents express doubts about the system. They are taken aback by the amount of strain and stress, the constant busyness and the fear of inspection. The teachers might be dedicated but their jobs are difficult.

> I think the vast majority of teachers are very dedicated and do a good job for the kids, whereas I said before I sometimes think they fall down with their relationships with other adults and…find them a bit threatening. (mother)

'Other adults' include inspectors and parents.

The relationship between parents and teachers will always be fraught because of the ultimate question of who is actually *in loco parentis*. At one level the question is absurd. Parents are the locus of control. At another level it is a difficult question. Of what are the parents in control? Do they have control of the children's learning, the acquisition of knowledge and the development of social skills? The way that the education system is designed and implemented by society suggests that parents have a lesser role to play. They hand over their offspring to experts who will tutor them according to the most up-to-date, most fashionable methods. Even the parents who would employ a private tutor would assume that the responsibility for education lays with the person employed.

The problem with this point of view is, of course, that it dissociates learning from the emotional understanding, the social insights, the motivations and the attitudes that lead to curiosity and certain paths of conduct and replaces it with testable skills and the acquisition of other peoples' knowledge and with conformity to public modes of behaviour. The very act of handing over a child into a closed community – closed to the outside world at least from nine until three – demonstrates a view of education that is narrow and impersonal. As teachers already know, the child comes to them already formed but treated as if they were blank slate. The myth is that schooling forms character, that the minor roles of teachers are, in fact, dominant. Teachers have the responsibility laid upon them, which is flattering, a burden and an essential misunderstanding. This misunderstanding enhances the prestige of the teacher and limits his power. Such a pressure of expectation can only lead to disappointment and disillusion. The greater the expectations of parents, the more attention is drawn to society's impersonal vision of the education system, a system in which teachers are servants not to the parents but to the state.

The separation of the development of personal relationships and understandings from the acquisition of knowledge and skills is itself a tragedy. It also places teachers in an intractable position. The result is that teachers tend to look, not to the parents but to the inspectors, not to their charges but to the curriculum. That sense of separation and the domination of a managed system – accountable, public, scrutinised and measured – puts teachers in a position of ambiguous power. No wonder they can be seen as distant, concentrating on their own survival and under strain. In these circumstances there is little opportunity or time for relationships with parents, let alone with their own pupils.

We see the result of this in the attitudes of teachers and parents. Teachers view the presence of parents with some alarm, with a mixture of suspicion and anxiety. They can be troublesome, time consuming and threatening. Parents are somewhat anxious about teachers, their authority, their command of the classroom and their power over children. The relationships are, as a result, often ambiguous. There is a great deal of warmth and respect on both sides, but never that closeness of mutual understanding that could bring so much benefit.

The way in which education systems have developed has perpetuated the separation of parents from their children, and made children schizophrenic between the societies of home and school. Each has different demands, far more disparate than those between the differences of work and play, or work and home for adults. Parents therefore find themselves observing their children adapting to different circumstances, and are to an extent marginalised. This affects their view of teachers.

Nevertheless, parents' views of teachers offer some telling insights. The sense of a distinction between the individual teacher, the individual school and the system as a whole is important and ironic since many of the parents' concerns are to do with the way the system is using teachers. The result of the circumstances is a view of teachers by parents that is a mixture of sympathy and critique. The educational system diverts teachers' attention away from parents. The irony is that this elicits parents' pity and understanding.

Parents acknowledge that teachers are better trained than they used to be, more professional in their approach and more aware of how to present themselves.

> I think teachers are better trained but they are encouraged to be less gifted. (father)

> I would say that they are better trained. I'm never quite sure what it means by professional for teachers. (mother)

Parents are impressed with the dedication, the hard work and the willingness for professional development. They see teachers using different skills than they did in the past, with more emphasis on the language of systems. Teachers are respected but it is a grudging admission that their job is more limited, at least in some instances.

> It depends on the area, you see. In the city the teachers haven't got time to think, let alone get a programme together. Here in this area, they're wonderful, they really are. (father)

The sense of admiration is always tinged with the image of burdens and problems.

> I think the teachers ... have had a lot to contend with but they are certainly as professional as they ever were ... so many good teachers. The thing is that they're suffering from overburdening bureaucracy. (father)

The two messages convey a sense of greater professionalism vitiated by greater bureaucratic demands. It could be suggested that the two things go together. The image of the teacher as the servant of the state, passing on the texts, arranging the successes and failures in the public exams and aware of the importance of presentation is certainly one interpretation of 'professional'. It suggests that bureaucracy, a term not used in a pejorative way, is essential. At the same time the parallel message is that of sympathy.

> To be honest, I don't know how some of the teachers cope with it. They don't need that extra pressure because they are already seen to be doing their best. I think there is more pressure on them than there used to be and they now have

a lot more training than there used to be. I know now they're as professional as they have ever been. (father)

The version of professionalism which parents detect is of the kind that stresses accountability and adherence to a set curriculum and uniform standards. It does not include the freedom of inspiration or spontaneity – all those memories most cherished by parents.

Despite the differences in the circumstances of parents in the sample, economic status – different parts of the country, inner city, suburban, rural – there were strikingly similar attitudes. Whilst these were complex and ambivalent, certain patterns emerged. One of the central notes that parents struck was their feeling for teachers under strain. They saw teachers, despite the excitement of the job, as suffering, beleaguered and pressured. They saw little pleasure in the delivery of the curriculum. Whilst not all teachers were admired, many of them were thought of as dedicated. They were often 'wonderful people'. But their job was no longer wonderful. It was viewed as impossible to do in a fulfilling way. Parents reiterated the stress that they observed.

I mean, I should think that the teachers put in a lot of hours. I mean, the hours the teachers have to put in, it must be very stressful for them. No wonder they get fed up with it. (mother)

In general, probably, I think they have more stress. I think it gets much more difficult and taking all that into account. They are probably hanging in there. (mother)

They all seem to be running around and doing a lot, but whether it's better I don't know. Because I think it is possible to achieve a lot without leaping around and appearing to be dashing around. Really inspired teachers, like our science teacher, who was not dashing around like a National Curriculum fiddler-abouter is now, he really engendered an excitement and interest in science. I should think that there is less of that and more hassle now. (father)

The sense that teachers are busy and under stress is ubiquitous. All the parents lay great emphasis on this. They use words like 'pressure', they point out that the pupils are becoming more difficult, they talk about 'new structures'. Above all, they pity the teachers, their being overworked and constrained, under greater control and without real autonomy. They are more professional in the pejorative sense of the term, a point of grudging admiration. But most of all, this greater dedication to the rigours of the job strikes parents as bewildering.

Parents feel that teachers have lost out in a number of ways. They feel that they have lost the excitement of their jobs. They have less time to teach in the real meaning of the term. Despite the professionalism that is attached to them, teachers have essentially lost status. The more distance that has been created from parents, the more respect is lost.

> They have lost status. They say they have lost motivation, enthusiasm. (mother)

Are these views of teachers, so highlighted by centralist policies, really new or do they reflect the more traditional position of teachers. Parents have an ambiguous view of teachers. Memories of their own subordination will fuel a spurious kind of respect. The concern with the well-being of their own children will create a sense of dependency and hope. Sympathy with what the teacher is trying to do will always be mitigated by the distance of the official. Parents place their own most personal property in the territory of others. They do this in the faith that is the right thing to do, as a means of fitting their children into society and its demands, both competitive and personal.

Parents also submit their most precious possessions into the hands of others because this has become the standard norm. This is what society as a whole has come to assume is right. Parents work whilst their children also work on preparing to work. By the parents' ambivalent submission to the demands of society, they not only distance themselves from what the teachers are doing but give the education system a particular slant. The clearest result of the acceptance of the system as it has evolved is not only the separation of the interests of the parents and teachers, but the dominance of the state.

8

The ethos of schools

Schools are distinct and peculiar institutions. In many ways they are an anomaly, out of date, inappropriate and part of the system that can cause as much damage as good. Every teacher will know the strangeness of school, in its unnatural implications and the tendency to bring out the worst in people, both in the atmosphere of the playground and in the fear that pervades the classroom. Pupils learn a lot about society and much that they learn is damaging. So far so bad, and teachers are inherently aware of this. They are engaged in mitigating, in putting right the system cultivated to suppress, rather than fulfil, the expectations of all the people in it.

But, and this is a big but, schools are not only a parody in miniature of society as a whole but create the possibility of real communities. The pupils learn from the examples they are set, and much of their complicated experience depends on how the school works as a community. On the one hand they see the power of hierarchies, the anxieties of inspection and all the worst aspects of managerialism. On the other hand they witness the care, the concern, the support and the vocation of people who bring about and foster the best aspects of their potential in understanding and in behaviour.

The school is an institution. Like many institutions the people in it behave according to the overall ethos, that connection between the leaders or managers and all the others. This can entail organisations where people are divided against each other, the sense of fear and isolation and all the typical aspects of incipient bullying that affects so much managerialism.

The school is also a community. Much depends on the head teacher, and this is a more complex matter than the kind of tactics promoted by politicians. Teachers need support, and need to be part of an understanding community to be effective. The school as a community needs to resist external pressure and it also needs a deliberate policy of mutual support. The school can be powerful if it has a collective vision and a strong belief in shared values.

Most teachers have experienced different schools, some of which are a pleasure to work in and others which are more like a nightmare. The pupils have no such comparisons and do not know what is possible. If they experience the brutality of the command structure and the official harassment of staff, they will conclude that this is what society is like. The deepest lessons that pupils learn have little to do with the National Curriculum. They learn about what they are always interested in from the beginning: the meaning of human behaviour. They can learn it in a terrifying way or destructive one. They can see how people are capable of giving mutual support and encouragement and they can also see the opposite. It is this, the essential experience of human behaviour and values that influences them more deeply than anything else.

No teacher is simply an individual acting alone. Any sense of isolation or alienation is destructive not just to the feeling of self-worth and the practice of teaching but to the effects that are inflicted on the pupils. The connection with the pupils might appear paramount and that is what teachers say is the saving grace of their jobs, but even more important are the relationships with other members of the school community. Whilst it might sound as if pupils are secondary, in a way they often feel they are, the real message of school and its essential purpose is how the staff works as a whole. It is from this that pupils learn. If the teachers feel there is mutual support and a shared understanding, they will naturally be far more engaged in explaining, in caring and in the way they respond to pupils.

A new teacher will be most conscious of the class, busy in preparation, obsessed by control, and worried about having something to say to the pupils. The real concern should be with the other teachers, the atmosphere of the staff room, the sharing of anxieties. As teachers become accustomed to the task of teaching they cease to worry so much about organising the pupils; this becomes so natural that they do not have to worry about the contents of their lessons. They instinctively realise that what matters arises out of the pupils' curiosity and that the art of teaching is more about response than instruction. What makes the real difference is the sense of support from a community of like-minded people. It is this that pupils perceive and which affects them profoundly. The targets and the assessment of the content of the curriculum are secondary issues.

In a school where the teacher can feel comfortable there is a shared vision of purpose. It is not something that can be imposed on the community like a mission statement but the result of an explicit desire by all involved to outline their values. Pupils learn about these things inadvertently; they need to have the sense of purpose made clear. In the research that explores the ethos of school and what that term actually means, it is clear that at the heart of any good school, like any organisation, lies a mutual belief in values. Compared to this the curriculum and the official policy statements, with their neutrality in terms of values, are not very significant. Making clear what the staff is trying to achieve, affects pupils' understanding more than anything else. This depends on two factors. The first is the importance of everyone in the school being equally involved in formulating the shared beliefs. It is not something imposed. The second factor is the realisation that a community is something that is organic and which depends on everyone in it. To acknowledge that the leader cannot create a change by sheer insistence or demand is a significant starting point.

Part of the culture of managerialism, that has done so much mischief, is the belief that one powerful figure can create effective changes resulting in a cult of control which aims to hit targets and squeeze outputs. It is as if there were certain factors, learned by the book that should make a fundamental difference. One day this mythology will be despised, since any leadership role is far more subtle, more personal and more co-operative but we have to live in a time when the myth of control is still prevalent, even if unsuccessful.

Teachers need to know that what counts more than league tables, competition, targets, results, accountability and all the measurement of compliance is the more complex community in which they move. It means that they should not be frightened of questioning. It means that the good managers are part of a team that talks about shared values. Every good head teacher of integrity has two things in common. The first is that they like people; other people and not just themselves. The second is that they have a firm belief in the collective success of their institution and consider themselves devoted to the people within the school rather than those outside. They consider themselves as mavericks fighting the worst absurdities of external control or interference. A strong school is a community, and can resist outside intervention if it believes in what it is doing.

Thoughtful head teachers lament the fact that their own staff take the statutory orders seriously. It might sound wilful to say that the targets, the systems and the tables should be ignored, but the irony is that success, even in the terms of measurable outcomes, depends on not taking them at face value. The reality of learning is more complicated, and relies far more on the values of the community than the adherence to the will of those who demand compliance. Teachers are not always aware that they do not have to comply with every directive they receive. If teaching is carried out simply to fulfil the requirements of official orders, the result is counterproductive. Targets can have a debilitating effect, often reducing standards, since because they have only to be met, once they are reached, they are no longer a spur to continue.

Teachers do not always readily stand up to external impositions. This underlines the importance of the community. The collective concern with real values is a necessary support to individual teachers. There is an important distinction between compliance, which is a danger to teachers, and collective concern to work together for mutual values. Pupils are very quick to detect the difference. The teacher who is seen to be doing things because he or she ought to, or has to because there is a fear of the consequences of external controllers, is rapidly detected. Pupils observe and analyse what goes on. They know what happens in the staffroom.

Whilst schools seem to depend on the organisation of the classroom, the real heart lies elsewhere. What happens in classrooms is within the context of a wider, more general, culture. The classroom is a small part of a larger assembly of people and the opportunities of interaction are far more significant outside. The classroom can feel like something separate, it can be tightly controlled but it is not separate. The classroom can be understood as a series of secret interactions, as a small society in itself, full of details of ritual and misunderstanding, but it is also affected by all that happens outside.

If there is an essential part of the school it is the staffroom. This is ironic, in so far as the purpose of the school, as well as the largest number of participants, focuses on the pupils. When pupils point out that school seems to them to be structured for the benefit of teachers they are revealing their acknowledgement of the centrality of what takes place amongst the staff. Staffrooms are the crucial factors in the school, not the head teacher. It is how well a staffroom functions that distinguishes a school with a committed sense of purpose from one where divisions, 'balkanisation' and the undermining of mistrust dominate. As one teacher who left the profession said, 'It was not the classroom I left. It was the staffroom.'

In their clear sighted (if often unexpressed) way the pupils also depend on the atmosphere of the staffroom. The heart of any school is the shared vision. This naturally entails many ambiguities which need to be recognised. The strongly held sense of purpose should not be conceived like an imposition on the pupils; they should be included in it. At the same time it is the staff's mutual support that matters. The teacher knows that the ideal is responsiveness rather than imposition. This means that in the institution of the school, shared values and mutual support amongst teachers is crucial. The pupils need to see this to share in the values. The involvement of pupils in shared values is not met by the tokenism of setting up a school council for occasional meetings, not a matter of committees and more rules or orders, but the daily practice of working out what matters and which engages everyone. Listening to pupils is not a way of getting them to comply more easily but an engagement in relationships and understanding. The results are long term, but the effects are immediate.

It is only when there are shared values with explicit outcomes that some of the ambiguities of the role of teachers and schools can be resolved. Like the contradictory interpretations of the word 'respect'. It can mean an acceptance of authority, the submission to superior experience and worth, or an assertion of personal independence. A well-functioning school knows that both have to exist, that courtesy to others is returned and understood, and is a place where every individual is cared for but where those with greater understanding and wisdom are recognised. Respect ultimately depends on the self, on the lack of defensiveness.

The problem for teachers is that the system as a whole is fundamentally dysfunctional. It works against all those principles that are most important. It is contrary to the way that pupils learn. It undermines the means that enable us to share learning, the true role of teachers, and the atmosphere of support in which teachers can flourish. But the system is powerful and teachers are aware of this. Despite all the good they do, protecting the very system that undermines them, they continue to be made to feel unimportant, but it is in the eyes of parents and pupils that they retain their worth. It is only in the eyes of those administrators who wish to control that the work of teaching is misunderstood.

When teachers are not respected enough to have ownership of what they do, then there are particular dangers. When the pressure is too much, teachers are tempted to react in two ways. The first is camouflage, hiding from reality. They pretend they are coping even when they are not, since the fear of not being able to survive drives them. They become accustomed to camouflage by seeming to fulfil all the tasks, by concentrating on the proofs of their trivial efficiency. They create material specifically against the chance of inspection. They cover up and soon find themselves disguising what they are really doing. The camouflage is forced upon them because they want to hide from the problems. One of the reasons that there is little said about how teachers cope is because they hide the circumstances even from themselves.

In this they are not unlike their pupils. There are matters that are kept secret, but no one dare say it, except privately. Teachers are associated with the state, with the policies that have such a formidable array of advertising and media coverage. Their unions are divided and, as in many institutions, more set on undermining each other than working for the common good. This criticism is the recognition that any oligarchy has to, like an academic subject, define itself against others and show how exclusively and separately it functions. Any ambiguity of role or effect which comes about through collaboration does not fit the standards of measurement and comparison. In a society that believes that the best results derive from competition, even public benefits become secondary. The pupils witness this marginalisation of their own teachers. They recognise the teacher's sense of powerlessness. And the more they sense it the more teachers want to camouflage their helplessness, trying to conform even when they know it is wrong.

Hiding the fact that they are dealing with a system with which they cannot cope begets camouflage. Teachers then also hide what good they are doing, and conform, at least in a reactive way, as if they feel they are powerless to resist. Camouflage is one temptation, one way of trying to cope.

Worse than camouflage is the temptation of collusion. It is hard to avoid, since there are statutory powers that insist on the wrong things. The rules are against teachers' principles. The evidence demonstrates that the more autonomy teachers have the better the results. Collusion means sacrificing the integrity of their position for its possibility of advancement, for personal profit. Again, there are links with the experience of pupils. Pupils are also forced to submit, to come to accept what they are required to do, even if is against their own best interests. Teachers are assumed to be in collusion with the general policies which is why it is refreshing to pupils to experience something different, more idiosyncratic, something far more individual. Sometimes collusion can mean basic dishonesty like making sure that the test results are constantly on the rise, and asserting continual improvement.

Collusion is a matter of accepting that targets make sense, that there is something measurable in the whole enterprise. Targets were a peculiar phenomenon. They are a way of imposing authority. They sound good. Targets depend on what can be easily measured and this is not just limited but contrary to the expression of different kinds of intelligence.

What teachers do cannot be measured. In the curious obsession with tables and targets, the idea of what is objective has become obscured. One table that carries the assurance, on precise and exact figures, that an institution is in the top place on Monday can be as easily presented, with equal authority, as showing the same institution as the lowest the next day. The many controlling attempts to fit accountability into targets always face their own nemesis of plausibility. The only targets that can be created within the meaning of the term – being measured and scrutinised for accuracy – have little validity. As with multiple choice tests the results are at best crude. Devotion to the accession of targets reduces performance to the lowest common denominator. Standards become an excuse for deficiencies since the need to demonstrate success inevitably means that a target must be within easy reach.

The attempts to create false objectivity cannot succeed because, although the performance tables of different institutions might look similar in terms of outcome, an institution is unique, something that cannot be recreated. It is constantly changing, dependent on too many variables to lend itself to simple summary. It is important for teachers to remember this. It is well known that league tables of schools depend on location. Leafy suburbs do surprisingly well compared with inner-city schools. And yet there is spurious fascination with league tables, that has become an international phenomenon. The ranking of departments or subjects, the idea of measurement, invoking accountability are still taken as an accurate sign of what is going on. It is another sign of collusion that people put up with it. There are great differences between what works and what does not, but the systems of measurement play no part in true judgement.

The problem for teachers is that this measurement becomes a distraction from the little time left for real reflection. What is measured is not the success of teaching or even the progress of pupils but the assessment of targets. The constant stream of new initiatives means that teachers are under pressure; this has undermined not only time but self-confidence. With the attack on self-confidence the very idea of professionalism is undermined.

> Although it is supposed to be a profession…I see it more and more as a job of work. I think a lot of the professional responsibilities have been taken away. (co-ordinator of mathematics)

The demands for a constant response to outside pressure means the teacher's core activity itself is under threat.

> There was a stage when we were doing … reports. I thought with a shock: 'Oh no I've got to teach now'. It shouldn't be like that. (head of art)

The conclusion that research comes to is that the whole system operates only because teachers are doing things they are not supposed to do, to keep it going. These illicit matters are the real gestures of helping individuals, giving advice, real teaching rather than the mechanical routines that are supposed to take place. The distractions based on testing the competence of teachers and assuming that they cannot be accountable to themselves simply undermine the point of teaching whilst pretending that it is the only way of mastering the system. Note the way in which the idea of accountability is mixed with measurement; for the underlying motivation is to seek out blame, to find faults.

The fact that teachers are controlled is not new, although the external constraints are greater and the power of constant surveillance is increased. What has been constant over the years is the power of hierarchies and the pressure to conform. Schools are collegiate places where so much depends on the interactions between people in them, but they are also places where the other side of collegiality – control – can make individuals subservient.

Given that the difference between what actually happens and what is seen to happen (and can be measured), the pressure to adapt to conformity is much stronger. When the head teacher is beleaguered by outside pressure then the same controlling instincts of conflict are passed on to heads of departments and then all the rest of the staff. What pupils observe is an unthinking conformity, a response to pressure, a fear of not meeting particular targets. The objective way in which pupils see this leads them to the conclusion that, whilst they are the raison d'être of the system, they are not really central to it. Teachers want to be effective but also have to convince other people and their pupils that they are so. They become part of a system in which all can be manipulated in the competition for results.

The irony behind all this conformity is that it is carried out in the name of market forces. The political takeover of the educational establishment was based on developing a contract; making schools like businesses and forcing them to be fully accountable to their customers. The inspectors were there to ensure that no bad business practices would take place and the public would have an insight into what schools were doing.

The culture of market forces and accountability depends on managerialism, a way of perusing objectives attractive to the management team but which are not necessarily beneficial to the shareholders. Thus, the positive ethos of a school that depends on shared values can be an artificial insistence on following instructions and meeting set targets. Teachers feel that their influence is diminished and their power severely constrained, just when the opposite should be the case.

As a result of these insidious forces teachers tend to hide what they really do, to submit with a vehement, if suppressed, resentment to the given system but secretly adhering to the real virtues of teaching. The system, ironically enough, could not survive without teachers doing all the extra work between the demands of official conformity. Both the conflict of interest and the pressure make the resulting experience very frustrating for teachers. The result is that teachers camouflage what they really do. It is hard to stand up to such pressure to conform to the standard demands and the threat of inspection. As a head of department said, 'You're made to feel unprofessional if you don't do these things'. When teachers talk about their experience of schools they articulate a range of responses. They mention seeking certainty in their teaching lives and some degree of control over their experience. They recognise that they have to compromise and develop a coping strategy to do so. They also camouflage difficulties or disguise anything they find unsatisfactory. They are aware of a constant sense of collusion between senior and middle managers and classroom colleagues. This summary of teaching is quite different from the ideal and certainly takes away the best kind of relationship with pupils.

The idea of learning that is expressed by pupils, that is yearned for and which makes the art of teaching both rewarding and valuable, depends on responsiveness and knowledge, or adaptability and spontaneity rather than the set targets. One could argue that in the school system such relationships have always been fundamentally difficult but the conditions have deteriorated over the years. This particular idea of what the teaching system should be like from a political perspective – manipulative, controlled, inspected without any real concern with the consequences – affects pupils deeply. They are the ones who suffer most since they are in no position to question it; if you know something is wrong it is easier to resist. The problem for teachers is that whilst there is a general acknowledgement that the manipulative system does not work, it continues in its absurd way and all the acknowledged failures are blamed on the teachers. The teachers almost do not dare to criticise or stand up for themselves, despite all the evidence. This is partly because very few people can accept the idea of a fundamental alternative based on quite different principles. Once confronted with an accepted norm it takes courage and knowledge to challenge the received assumptions. But this also affects teachers who should be in a better position to resist.

When teachers talk of their experience they echo many of the points that pupils make. The comments include statements such as, 'The number of times I've said in the last three years that teaching is an incidental part of my day…'. The more teachers are distracted by constant demands, difficult to define and harder to justify, the more they feel that they are lurching from crisis to crisis rather than in control. The question remains why teachers should put up with such a system.

Perhaps the dangers of collusion are best highlighted in a series of small examples in which teachers are pressured to conform in ways that are dishonest but are equally taken for granted as necessary by those in control of the system. In one department it was agreed that to increase the school's league table position the 'middle band' students should acquire a least a grade 'C' at GCSE. The department insisted that all the teachers' efforts should be placed on one set of pupils because this would have the biggest impact on the league table position. 'We are just concerned with the middle band … To get them there, because it is going to look good.' The other pupils were to be left to their own devices since the target did not include them.

In another incident, year eight reports had been completed and passed to form tutors for checking and signing. Because of the absence of a member of staff one department had written a generic report detailing what work they had done. The form tutor was instructed to tick the effort and attainment boxes even though he knew nothing about any of the pupils. 'Well, at least they are done.' But then the reports that teachers have to fill, justifying or asserting what they have taught (rather than what they think the pupils have learned) are so standardised, so bland as to be of no interest to parents. The parents long for the informal word from the teacher, instead they are supposed to put up with the lengthy, time consuming, and meaningless details of the new official reports.

Such concerns with fulfilling tasks can be demonstrated in a situation in which certain teachers had completed a series of annual student reports. They had to choose comments from a bank of statements and code them. These codes were entered into a computer by administrative staff and the report was generated for signing by the teachers. They were instructed to 'sign the report in blue ink. We don't want it to look as if the report was photocopied'.

In a system in which the school has to judge its results against a set of criteria – and make sure that there is steady progress rather than any fluctuation in test results – there will be many other prerequisites and demands other than the welfare of pupils. The external constraints are clear and demands on teachers to conform to them equally so.

Schools are always organisations in which the twin demands of internal coherence and external presentation will be paramount. The individual learner is expected to conform. What makes this system far worse than others is the extent of external monitoring and control. The autonomy of the school is paramount and can be a good or bad thing. Reports on the fate of schools demonstrates the necessity of the freedom of the school and individual teacher. The sense of personal ownership is crucial

Schools depend on their autonomy from external controls and constraints and teachers need to understand this. When a school is dictated to from the outside, it is never as successful, or as fulfilling, as it should be. Teachers feel uncomfortable with this conformity and need the collective courage to know that it can be resisted. There are many external influences on the school. Specifically, parents. More generally and just as powerful, is the general culture and what is going on in the community. But these external influences are counter to the attempts to control and organise the delivery of targets and performance indicators. The problem for teachers is that they are aware of this. But teachers do not know quite how to act on this knowledge.

One reason for this desire to control from outside might be the doctrine of market forces and accountability. The implementation through inspection is one of its main products. This will always have a deleterious effect on standards, since those things which can be measured and compared at will only consist of those matters that will limit themselves to the constraints of tests. If the research on the best ways for schools to operate is consistent, then so is the research that looks at the effects of inspection. Whether it is pupils or teachers that are being measured, the tendency is to find those things that could be targeted; these will be less and less demanding and more achievable. Inspection reduces the options and spontaneity of a teacher and the very fact of inspection limits the kind of preparation a teacher might make. Apart from anything else, the teacher has to spend time preparing to be inspected.

The effect of inspection for pupils, however, goes far deeper (Cullingford 2008). The teachers have to perform to the demands of visitors, preparing the paperwork, practicing lessons, making sure everything is in order, but they do this pragmatically, if fearfully. They might think that such an inspectorial regime, when the strangers have power and can conclude what they wish – they are not themselves accountable – is punitive, threatening and stressful (Winkley 1999). This is simply the most extreme manifestation of external control, the exaggerated display of the power of the state to enforce its policies, to police its intentions. The teachers tend to be put under great strain, since they do not always know the motivations behind the inspections. Even internally there are tensions. The inspection can be used by a head teacher to make radical and innovative changes. So the inspection can be used for good if it presents a needed opportunity, since it presents a weapon. Teachers will use anything to hand. But this is the sign of a school knowing what it wants; it can use the inspection. The inspection in itself rarely gives any insight that the teachers are not aware of already.

The inspection, however it is handled, is bound to be vibrant with friction and distress. But it remains simply the example of external control, the attempt to make sure that teachers comply with requirements. The school does not necessarily have to conform in such a rigid way, although it tends to do so in a pragmatic manner since it will take whatever is useful and ignore the absurd elements. The strain of the teacher is yet more paperwork, more writing everything up, more careful attention to every piece of written evidence that can be inspected. The inspection will always have its limitations. It is to comply with a formula and it is about the school out of context with its circumstances. But it is accepted as an inevitable part of the state system.

However stressed, teachers generally take a practical attitude to the inspection. The damage done to individuals is resented and the bullying implicit in such an approach is deplored by the teachers.

For the pupils, the experience is fundamentally different. They might not appear to care and they continue with their usual routines. They see their role, if necessary, to support the teachers who might ask them to do certain things. The pupils know exactly what is going on; what games are being played. All the time they observe very closely. They might be silent witnesses but these are formative occasions. The pupils learn some fundamental lessons from the inspection.

The first lesson is that bullying is not just a school-age phenomenon. It is government policy. The pupils see the teachers under strain, they witness the nervousness and the fear. They know that something unnatural is going on. Here is the example of systematic control by the implementation of fear, the example of not trusting teachers, of insisting on conformity. Outsiders have the right of entry into the teachers' domain, at least for a short time, and have to make a judgement from which a full, formal, public report is drawn. That is the official line; what the pupils observe is the abject position of their teachers and where real power lies. Whilst the inspectors would deny that bullying was ever the intention – 'People have to be accountable and poor teachers named and shamed' – this is what pupils learn about the society in which they live. They learn about political fashion in a practical way. They realise how little power the teacher has compared to those who control the system.

However short notice the inspectors have, the teachers are also seen immediately to prepare. The inspection is not a natural occurrence. It demands paperwork, the scrutiny of every aspect of the school that can me measured and written up. Teachers rehearse for the occasion and a well-run school will carefully adapt, using every device to make sure that their school is at its best. If ever there were days in which pupils are pleaded with to behave better than normally these are they. So the pupils learn about 'spin'. It is not what you do with that counts but how you present yourself. The greater the preparation the more unnatural is the actual event. Pupils learn the ways in which people ready themselves for formal situations, how they officially camouflage and collude in the system. Pupils are given ready access to cynicism, an insight that is hard for teachers to break down, especially if they defend such a regime.

Pupils, therefore, gain two major insights into the culture in which the schools are embedded. Whether this is the intended message or not, such an inspectorial regime undermines their teachers in the eyes of the pupils. If teachers attempt to control them into working harder, or achieving higher standards, this is often interpreted as simply a concern for the tables and hitting targets. If teachers seem to care for their pupils they are also deemed to be essentially under the control of the inspectors and having to care more for themselves and their careers than the well-being of their pupils. In the culture of individualism and competitiveness even the most self-sacrificing of people lose something of their authority. The cynical pupils are supported in an assumption that the teachers only do what they do, however good, because they are fearful of what would happen if they did not do so.

To some extent this kind of undermining has always been part of the school; the system in which teachers operate is more significant than their place as individuals, mentors and guides. Schools have hierarchies surrounding them as well as being hierarchies in themselves. The central focus is not on the pupils learning but on results from a performance which can be measured.

In their need to learn, pupils are sensitive to all the messages that they receive, including the negative ones. Their attitudes toward society and their futures in it are formed by a variety of influences and most of these are inadvertent. The hidden curriculum of tacit assumptions is far more subtly powerful than the official offerings.

Even before they go to school pupils are aware of social context and of reputations. They realise that there are strong attitudes in their communities, not so much to them as individuals but to the schools they attend, whether they have made it somewhere 'satisfactory' or whether they attend a 'sink' school. Whilst parents are desperate to make sure their offspring enter a good school, their concerns and fears have an effect on the pupils.

> I heard lots of rumours and my brother used to come here so he used to tell me all these things that used to happen. The used to send you the wrong way if you asked directions and things. (girl, year 10)

Older siblings and friends are notorious for passing on messages not just about the school but about individual teachers. It is the general reputation of the school, and its ethos, that matters. While some might think that it is only the results that dominate, the pupils are far more sensitive to the general atmosphere of the school.

This term 'atmosphere' might seem vague but everyone who works in an institution, let alone any school, will know how important such a concept is. Large-scale studies of schools have depended heavily on the idea of an 'ethos'. A sense of shared belief and purpose affects all the people in it, and is detectable in policies and in the way people interact with each other. Those places in which people look forward to work are different from those where every day is dreaded or resented. It is clear that ethos dominates (Rutter *et al.* 1979, Mortimore *et al.* 1988). When they talk about school pupils they are very concerned with what they call (without awareness of the research) a 'friendly atmosphere' and a 'working atmosphere'.

Friendly atmosphere, meeting my friends, and getting on with people...I do like the school. (girl, year 10)

Pupils might feel individually marginalised in the intricacies of school and its beleaguered position in response to external demands, but they know what they would want from a school. They dread a 'factory routine' (girl, age 15). They want to be treated 'like an adult'. They learn to resent the fact that they have no voice, that individual learning is nothing compared to the demands of their conformity. Pupils feel themselves a small part of a larger regime. The extent to which they feel individually protected and cared for is of immense importance.

One thing is clear to them. They are not, and presume they will not, be protected by the community. This sense of being 'on your own' pervades both the academic and social sides of school. Pupils feel exposed rather than protected; they dread being 'picked on' either for poor work or poor behaviour. It is this social experience that makes the school even more important than the academic one. School can be a protected environment, and should be at a time when the pupils are confidently expanding their understanding. But schools are often places where pupils are afraid rather than secure.

What pupils would like from education

The essential axiom remains. People love to learn but resent being taught. But how deep is the desire to learn and what does it mean? When one is confronted with recalcitrant pupils who seem to have everything else on their mind but the task in hand, to remember that there is an essential human need to acquire knowledge seems remote. Nevertheless, we know from all the research, that the need, and not just the desire, goes deep and is shared by everyone, however brutalised and hidden it might have become.

There are certain things that we know very well about young people. The first is the sheer capacity and the speed of early learning, the acquisition of new ideas and vocabulary, the perception of people's ideas and the analysis of the environment. This speed of learning depends on the power of the brain. This early ability is a challenge as well as a demand.

Knowing about the capacity of the brain, and the ability of certain people to exploit it, leads to a challenge for teachers. The challenge is to understand the implications of such power. If the early years are so formative they are so in the circumstances in which the person grows up. Culture, religion and language all depend on the cultural environment. This is an aspect of globalisation; the knowledge of other people, their differences, and antipathies, and the dominance of tribalism that should lead to a recognition of the importance of the formative powers of education, much more deeply than the acquisition of skills. To say that everything depends on genetics is to falsify the reality of every day life. People think and speak according to the language and attitudes around them. Human nature might have certain fundamental attributes but it is only expressed in terms of certain kinds of conduct, certain kinds of thinking and certain kinds of understanding according to the circumstances.

If we know about the power of learning we also know something about how people react to the way learning opportunities are presented to them. The first hint is clear and that depends on the circumstances. There is a large mythology about learning styles as if each person can only endure a particular form of presentation, but this is a very superficial and often meaningless way of the noting individual differences. The real essentials about how people learn are more individual and more cultural; they depend on certain attitudes which give an insight into the great difference between the power of learning and the passiveness of being 'talked to'.

The first important insight into learning is the sheer absorption of new information. A very young child observes and retains all of his or her experiences. There is a process of a very fast assimilation of views, feelings and attitudes according to the circumstances in which they are experienced. The context is all and this context is a constant attempt to define and make sense of a mass of conflicting information.

Also crucial is the power of discrimination. Young people are very good at understanding the concept of number, almost from the beginning. Numbers are a way of categorising things. Without this mental form of measurement and without categories the understanding of the mass of information would be too great. All thought needs organisation. There are different perspectives, different ways of definition, and soon the categorisation of the world begins to be very important. Words like 'big', 'far', 'wide' or 'long' all have the same sense of weight and potency but they are, according to the context, very different in meaning. Categories, and the power to categorise, the ability to make sense of things so that numerous individual objects become both whole and separate, are at the heart of this power of discrimination.

Together with the power to absorb and the power to discriminate comes the personal meanings, the idiosyncratic interpretation of what takes place. This is where emotional sympathy, the understanding that other people have their own points of view and that they can deceive, are all important. Each individual has to learn in his or her own way, according to the information that is given to them. They are not passive receivers of ideas or facts but are people who have to create a personal meaning from all that they receive.

This suggests that the discriminating and absorbing mind is constantly seeking to make sense of experiences and that these experiences are much more than the simple accumulation of other people's facts and other people's ideas. Learning is not the same as being taught.

There are three ways in which young children learn. The first is by association, by making connections between things and ideas. This is a process both of categorisation and of memory and extrapolation. The importance of associations should not be underestimated. It is the ability of the mind to connect different ideas, to understand whether connections should be made and to come to certain logical conclusions from the various pieces of information stored in the brain.

At the same time it should be noted that associations can be ultimately undermining in so far as certain memories and attitudes are triggered automatically by circumstances. It depends on whether the associations are to be encouraged as a means of creating a whole and deeper understanding of the world, or whether they are a kind of reversion to superficial impressions and automatic responses.

Associations are very important as a way of learning since they depend much more on what sense that the learner gives to the facts than the way the material is presented. The learner draws ideas together in a way that is always different from the way the presentation was originally made. Another form of categorisation is not just the first movement towards the concept of a word and an idea, but is also way of seeing the world, through the use of images. The images are evoked by meaning which is why stories are very important. Each person has his or her own image of what is being read – such is the power of fiction and communication.

Together with associations and images comes the ability to make judgements, to be critical. There is always an element of self-awareness and self-consciousness in the absorption of stories and ideas and this ability to hold back, to be not wholly or completely engaged in something is also powerful. Most people remember those transformative experiences when they were completely caught up in some other realm of imagination, these rare experiences when the importance of criticism and discrimination was temporarily suppressed.

When it is recognised that young people learn alone in a realm of their own this is not just a wilful or sentimental idea. There is a very deep need to explore imagination, almost a biological necessity, as described in neuroscience and cognition. Learning is at the same time a social and a private matter. Teachers need to understand this difference because they can foster but not dictate. Learning is, after all, a matter of personal understanding. If one can see pupils as people who really want to know, instead of people who are opposed to any kind of imposition then we can see the potential of the world in a different way. The puzzle remains why this fact is not grasped: the system of imposed learning casts a shadow on the desire to learn; if it is imposed long enough the desire to learn withers away.

What pupils want to learn is also very clear. They want to know why people are as they are. They are surrounded by all kinds of examples of behaviour and attitude. They relate closely to a few people in depth but they also seek to understand them.

They have exemplars of other people's ideas and attitudes. The question for them is why should people be so different and so individual?

This last question comes because what children also want to learn is concerned with why they are as they are. They understand aspects of personality. They have an instinctive grasp of the complexity of nature versus nurture and the fact that people are born with certain temperaments and are also conditioned by particular environments. Why is this? Why are they confronted with the conditions of where they are? What does this mean? To some extent all people are conditioned to be self-centred. All learning means something to them personally. It is not something abstract or given, but is something that tells them who they are and why they are the way that they are.

The crucial matter then is not the question of dull facts or mathematical logic, but how these are applied to them and the places in which they live. Even if absorbed in the pursuit of knowledge for its own sake, or a particular skill like that of playing the violin, it is the social world that forms them, that makes them aware. The crucial matter of learning depends on how people behave and how they come to behave in such a way. The heart of learning and understanding is conduct.

All these particular questions and ways of learning lead to the importance of intellectual relationships. Children and pupils have many relationships with many different kinds of people on an every day basis. Some are permanent and some are purely ephemeral. The way in which people relate to each other is the essence of life.

At the same time young children have very warm relationships. We know from the literature that the sheer warmth of an emotional attachment is not enough in itself. What matters to young people, with all the information that keeps bombarding them, is to make some kind of sense of it that relates to their own personal understanding. They cannot do this on their own even if the system assumes that they can. They need other people to help them make sense of all the experiences that they have.

The relationship that the young crave is not sentimental attachment to one or two people, but rather the need to share intellectual ideas, accept different points of view and share a vision of what is possible. When young people find their lives becoming meaningless it is because they have not had a relationship with the mind where they can see both the point of view of others and share their own. Learning is a matter of intellectual relationships with others. 'Others' can include books and experiences, praise and music to name just a few. This relationship is based on a shared dialogue with another mind, even if this is in written form. Nothing is so important for a young mind as the idea that he or she is exploring ideas with other people. The moment that other people are authoritarian and tell them what to think, that relationship is broken. The moment other people insist on their own experience and do not relate to others, the relationship loses its momentum. The moment that the desire to share a personal experience of learning with someone else is not fulfilled, there is a lack of satisfaction, a disappointment and the potential to undermine the whole idea of understanding.

Learning is not neutral. One can absorb a succession of facts but this can only be done if there is a motivation, if there is a reason. One can practice for hours at an instrument but little will be achieved if there is no desire towards an idea of mastery. Learning is an emotional and intellectual engagement with an idea or outcome that matters.

Pupils always learn, but they can also learn not to think, not to understand, not to accept other people and not to accept themselves. Learning is a very positive thing which needs nurturing, encouraging and extending. If it is not helped, it is something that will rapidly disappear. This disappearance is not just of the capacity to learn, but the desire and belief in learning. This disappearance is not just of learning itself but of the good that learning will do; people will replace the positive with the negative but will not remain neutral.

If learning is not a neutral matter but a case of engaging with information and ideas on the personal and emotional level, then it is also a moral issue. What concerns teachers has ultimately to do with values, with conduct and understanding. These are not matters of simple rules but matters of personal importance. The teacher cannot impose but can guide and respond appropriately. The teacher is also the example of good conduct. This includes not just behaviour but the tolerance and understanding of others and their points of view. A teacher will not respect all ideas, but will respect the people who hold opinions.

There have been many sayings are over the years about the ability to mould a young child. It is the first three years, so the research shows, that are of crucial importance and this is a time when learning is more subtle, not a matter of imparting beliefs.

The first requisite for an education system, therefore, is to concentrate on the support of parents and others involved in very young people's lives. What the very young need are the kinds of people who have an interest in them, who can talk with them, interact with them and share her pleasures with them. The stress should be on talk and should be concerned with the ideas that the young child expresses.

Stories are essential. A young child can only understand his or her world if it is put into some kind of coherent order. Events are important but the child understands these events by seeing them in context. But one does not need to force a child's attention; this is natural and needs to be encouraged. In the first three years, therefore, the two essential needs of a child are the relation of many stories and the provision of many books.

Nothing is more important than supporting parents, all parents. There should be large communities who are there are to support the role of parents. It is important to understand the difficulties of parenting and the needs for other people, like grandparents and anybody who is available, to help and to support. The first three years of an education system should be a systematic support for very young people and their parents and other relations.

The implication of this is that there would be many sites for learning. Museums, art galleries and libraries, any place which is filled up with interest of a kind that can be shared with adults, would be places where learning could take place. At a time when information is enhanced by computers, there is no longer an important difference between schools and other places that can provide access to that information. A site for learning is where people can talk and have iterative dialogue. Information is not enough in itself, though. If any place with access to the Internet can be used as a place where individuals learn this implies two things. In an ideal circumstance, from the point of view of the pupils, there would be no schools in their current form. Schools are unnatural devices, created at a time when there were few resources to convey information and when the need to instil information, like the ability to read, dominated. Schools are an outdated model and this is a fact that the teachers have to put up with. In an ideal learning environment all adults would become teachers, not by playing a role or by possessing information, but by interacting with the learning individual. If an education system could ever grasp this fact, the theatre of learning would indeed be transformed.

From the point of view of the learner, the whole emphasis of the education system would be on learning rather than being taught, on exploring rather than being controlled. Sharing ideas would not just be with peers, however convenient and however important, but with adults, as well. There would be lots of dialogue, lots of exploration of ideas, and a great deal of philosophy, of logical thinking, of questioning things. Above all, it would mean sharing ideas and having a sense of purpose. The natural desire to explore and read information, and make lists of what is known, would have a kind of purpose beyond the mere regurgitation of facts for the purposes of testing.

What strikes pupils at the moment about a school is its imposition, its rules, its sense of implacable governance. If the emphasis was on the responsibility of the individual to learn, to find the means of having dialogue and understanding, of pursuing a particular interest, then the nature of education will be radically different and the purpose of teachers that much more rewarding. They would be the centre of certain kinds of knowledge which they could share with those who wish to understand it.

All this suggests that the idea of testing skills, or attainments and targets, of having a whole system of curriculum laid out by a central political body, is beside the point. Will people question what happens to standards if we don't have this huge system? Standards would, if the emphasis of education were different, be so much higher. Education is a social matter, and the concentration on conduct and behaviour which underlies the reason for understanding, would be a transforming influence.

There are many unexamined assumptions about learning. One is that it is important to pursue all aspects of the curriculum, that the arts and the sciences must be equally explored and that a little bit of knowledge of everything is important. This is pure mythology. Pupils can learn perfectly well by pursuing one topic in great depth. On the one hand pupils find the notion of distinct 'subjects' absurd; on the other hand they are capable of pursuing one interest in great depth. If they have a gift like that for musical instruments or for mathematics, then it should be pursued as much as possible.

One reason pupils are put off some subjects is that each subject is presented in an equivocal way. On the one hand it is supposed to be important for its own sake, even if it seems to have no relevance to the pupils or no relationship to real life, and on the other hand it is obviously only a small part of a whole. The problem with a 'subject' is that it seems to be everything to those teaching it, and yet the curriculum spreads, broadly if not in a balanced way, around them all. Each subject fights for its position, so that the idea of knowledge is presented as a series of internecine battles, each other subject being by implication disparaged. The idea of 'doing' a 'central' subject seems absurd to pupils. They are forced to understand that there should be a core curriculum where certain matters are crucial. When they are made to undergo certain skills for their own sake and without any sense of purpose, then the very idea of a subject is very destructive. I would argue that the notion of a complete 'discipline', whilst very attractive in terms of complete command for the person involved, as if there could be complete control and mastery, has been a destructive force in the development of intellectual ideas. Let pupils pursue a topic that interests them and they will find that they can cover a huge variety of ideas.

The curriculum should be based on what most interests pupils. Pupils have two great concerns. The first is the real world in which they find themselves. They want to know how society operates and how it affects them. They also want know something about the reasons for people's individual and collective behaviours. If this is addressed, then all other kinds of human knowledge have a purpose and integrity that transforms any subject into something of real interest. If pupils pursue one particular topic that interests them, then they also wish to relate it to something which seems to them to be of extreme importance and significance. The real world is concerned with all kinds of manifestations of human endeavour and there is nothing purely abstract or separate. Every art is a consolation and way of understanding the world; every excitement in delving into a subject is driven by the realisation that it is getting closer to the essentials of human life.

The places that pupils would want to learn in are clear in their essential characteristics, however diverse. They are safe havens where they can rely on some essential factors. One is that they will have a sense of freedom from imposed rules and that the expectation of good conduct and courtesy to others is self-generated. All pupils complain that they feel at times that the school is like a prison. Once the whole idea of education is based on force rather than agreement, then that sense of oppression will be inevitable. Pupils want to feel that they are there because they want to be, and that makes all the psychological difference to their learning.

Such a sense that pupils are free to learn also puts a great deal of responsibility on them. It makes them understand that good conduct is essential, that standards are high, that the desire to learn must not only be nurtured but enabled in all the people near them. Freedom from a sense of oppression brings a sense, not of 'rights', but of the responsibility of having the chance to choose, be responsible and to be trusted. There is then no need to assert the rights of being treated seriously which come about as a reaction to being imposed upon or of 'respect'. This latter term is a cloak for self-assertion in the face of what is perceived as pressure to conform.

The other important point about the place in which to learn is that it should be of such a kind that that encourages dialogue. It must be intimate enough to be the natural site of conversation rather than silence, for when silence is needed for personal purposes, it has to be respected. In the normal circumstances of school, the silences are enforced and arbitrary. The prevention of conversation reinforces the idea of the prison, of rules imposed, of keeping people in order since they are assumed to be entirely recalcitrant if order were not constantly imposed. In the regime of schools, talking is discouraged for a number of telling reasons. One is that the silence is the representative of authority and that any other sound is that of rebellion. Another is that talking is somehow subversive, that there might be secret pleasure in it. The fact that pupils might learn a lot from each other and that they can find real group work constructive, goes against the febrile assumptions of imposed order in the classroom.

Talking also symbolises co-operation rather than competition. Schools can be very oppressive, not only because of the imposed rules, and the strictness of discipline, but more essentially because of the anonymity and lack of personal identity in the pupils. They might as well have numbers, like prisoners, so that the individual can be picked out for punishment. Competitions reinforces that banner: 'you are on your own', that idea of individual endeavour against others. Talking seems to symbolise the idea that learning is about exploring collective ideas, rather than testing facts.

Whilst there are many examples of the way in which the environment affects people, these come about because of, and not despite, certain human characteristics. Pupils have a profound, some might say, instinctive, sense of the psychology of human nature, including their own. Naturally, they have not been taught any of the terminology, not even psycho-babble, that would give them some kind of vocabulary. What they express comes not second hand, is not imposed or theoretical. What they perceive and talk about is the fragile balance between their own natures and the circumstances in which they find themselves.

They often wish they had been born under a happy star. They see certain people who are naturally blessed with a happy temperament and worry about their own.

In particular they worry about the burden of their own personality, the fact that they are prone to provocation, that despite themselves, they react with far more fervour than is warranted. They know themselves, and they know that each person is different.

At the same time they observe the results of poor upbringing. They see those who are being mishandled by their parents; they have no sympathy and are not sentimental about the dreadful effects of an intellectually and spiritually poor home. They will sympathise with the spiritual impoverishment that results in bad behaviour, but they will not therefore condone the effects.

Young people know about the tensions between personality and upbringing, between rights and responsibilities, and between the need for rules and the demands of conduct. Given such awareness, why do we not make more use of it?

There is no alternative. If we neglect young people's needs, then we quietly and unpleasantly create a society that diminishes human endeavour. The young are willing to learn all the basic truths about human nature, because they need to. By diminishing them and their power to learn we not only deny it to them but condemn the rest of humanity to something which at best is not satisfactory. All this is not inevitable.

Teachers should be care about humanity and its future. At the moment teachers mitigate and ameliorate the worst that the systems do to people. If they could be liberated from shoring up something that is not essentially right and turn to their deeper love of communicating their own learning, pursuing ideas and sharing their own interests, then we would return to the true idea of teaching, the tutorial, the pupils wanting to approach the teacher without being forced to. Meanwhile we have to hold on to the ideal, knowing that it remains that for the time being.

If we took young people's views more seriously, we would:

1. give them more support, from a variety of sources, in the early years;
2. give them many more places in which they could learn;
3. have many more people involved.

This would not only give meaning to individual lives, but make a difference to the lives of the whole.

CHAPTER

9

Intelligence
What teachers can do

The power of recognition

If we understand intelligence as a given, immutable ability, distributed unequally amongst the pupils, we are already in making an essential mistake. Given the educational system, the hierarchies, the league tables, the constant comparisons, it is difficult to avoid being influenced by the idea of innate ability of different people. We have to admit that stupidity is blatant and dangerous. But intelligence is a far more complex phenomenon. Intelligence should be thought of as active thinking, as the application of the mind. It is not just a latent ability, but dependent on the way it is fostered.

Intelligence is like the capacity for language. It is a human ability, but it depends on the particular environment. It is not only formed in the culture of the circumstances, but it depends on the extent to which it is cultivated. The mind grows according to the way it is used. Intelligence is always alive to conditions and demands. Intelligence, in whatever form it takes, is an essential human attribute, not something confined to a minority. Recognising this, and seeing the potential of each individual, is a prerequisite for teachers.

Children's emotional and physical needs are more strident than their intellectual ones, but not stronger. The curiosity to seek out new understanding and awareness needs fulfilment, and atrophies if it is denied. It appears sometimes as if all kinds of efforts, personal and social, are made to suppress it. Once it is denied, the confidence and motivation to think is not easily read regained.

It is a telling fact that on first entering the educational system all children seem to thrive. They exhibit real curiosity and excitement, a desire to absorb and a willingness to explore. After two years, this shared confidence fades away markedly in some, in those who have not learned to adapt to the demands of school. This can be interpreted as the result of earlier socio-economic deprivation, but it can also be understood as a limitation of the system of schooling.

Intelligence is complex. It takes many forms. It depends on the confidence to try, to guess, to experiment and to question. The skills of thinking are emotional and social and knowing this can empower teachers not only to believe in their pupils but to make a real difference.

The pupils' point of view

Children want to please. They know that they are obliged to fit into the demands of the school. They are taught to adapt. This makes them sometimes polite about their experience of school and sometimes mute. When we really try to explore their experience the intellectual frustration becomes very clear beneath the constraint, and the submission.

The children for whom the quotations illuminate what they think are not a carefully chosen sample. Whilst there are wide ranges of individual differences and experiences there are certain themes which stand out. There are many events, which all pupils experience in common, and it is the central consistency rather than the exceptions that we need to understand.

There are certain phrases that are familiar to all and which summarise school experiences. One of these is the dread command 'Do it again'. All the routines of school, the repetition of work, the fine tuning according to the strictness of demands are clarified. No one would suggest that work should not be made as good as possible or presented as a highly finished article. Indeed, drafting and redrafting is one of the essentials in any task that has an audience and an outcome. Pupils understand that and accept it, but that is not what they associate with 'Do it again'. This they think of as a demand for neatness or a way of filling up time. It can be invoked because they are too far ahead of the others or because they are falling impossibly behind. It seems to them often to be an encouragement of the routine without a clear purpose. It is often the result of not understanding what it is that the teacher wants.

The intellectual frustration of school is the realisation that there are certain demands and expectations and not knowing exactly what these are. Pupils appreciate the teachers who explain, who are clear, who can communicate. Yet all of them have experienced the bewilderment of not knowing what they are supposed to be doing.

Another universal outcry is 'It's not fair'. This is the symbol of frustration at the inbuilt injustice and arbitrariness of events. None of this unfairness is deliberate, but it is potent. It is a reflection of the realisation that there are some deep-seated disparities and of impossibility of making true judgements in the circumstances.

At the deeper level, pupils realise the distinction between effort and achievement. They know that to some pupils the set tasks come easily. They know what to do and can work fast and neatly. Others, for all their best endeavours, always seem to get things wrong. Their very frustration is cumulative, and undermining.

Another strand of unfairness comes from the volatility of rules and discipline. In the maelstrom of relationships, of quarrels and arguments, of blame and retribution, there is also a strong sense that justice should be done. This demand for fairness and justice is a difficult and challenging one, as in other walks of life, and yet the cases where the wrong person is picked on, and the innocents punished, seem, to pupils, to abound. Again, this is inadvertent. Given the circumstances, no one has time to sort out individual cases and delve into each circumstance. The rules mean arbitrary, quick decisions or, worse, a deliberate ignorance of what goes on.

These social events have intellectual consequences. They distract from the excitement of thinking. The routine work, 'Do it again', contrasts with the alternative curriculum of relationships, the causes of behaviour, and the sharing of ideas.

Those pupils who are exposed as not keeping up easily lose their intellectual self-confidence. Those who were not listened to or not taken seriously soon become frustrated and cease to try. Those who do not have the reasons for decisions explained to them feel disenfranchised. In such circumstances, it is difficult for intelligence to flourish.

First understand the problem

Highlighting the difficulties pupils and teachers face is one way of celebrating what is possible, even if frustrated by the whole system of policies. Most teachers do a remarkable, even impossible, job in the circumstances which could more easily diminish and undermine them. Whilst it might suit a few to adapt to the bureaucracies of schooling and inspection, it is not the same as the joy of seeing pupils' potential and developing them. Concentrating on the problems is not to be negative. On the contrary, this is to celebrate what is possible and what remains undimmed. Understanding the facts about intelligence and potential is itself a powerful weapon. It explains the frustration with all the distractions from teaching and connects it to the everyday experience of teachers. This is no ideal state, but a real one.

The problems that pupils face affect them all. They are not confined to a few, the gangs, the disillusioned or the perennially miserable. Once one employs a 'typology' of failure or success, of victims and bullies, of jokers and goodies, one is already in some difficulty. As is the case with bullying, we are aware of the extremes, of those who are always in trouble. The real problem, however, lies in the witnesses, the majority, who put up with things, who turn a blind eye. Most of the pupils who have difficulties make no fuss about them. They take for granted that these are part of school life. Some try to disguise their unhappiness from others and some even from themselves. It does not have to be like this.

Whilst there are some pupils who make their discontent plain, and who receive a disproportionate amount of attention, most remain quiet, almost invisible. They submit, they quietly get on with their set tasks, they try to be as anonymous as possible. Whilst it is those who play truant and become excluded who cause major difficulties and take up time, there are many more pupils who are psychologically excluded, who seemed to conform and make no trouble, but who have long ago given up.

Every child should be the centre of attention, which is why it is important to see and hear all pupils, without excluding any. We see their individualities when we see the baselines of difficulties. The problems we need to understand can the outlined in five different ways.

1. There is the conflict between one kind of thinking, one form of intelligence, and the demands of another form of expectation. The spirit that the pupils want to bring to bear rests on exploration, on asking difficult questions, in taking risks with ideas and in scrutinising their own worlds in all its many layers. They are then faced with a curriculum that demands their submission to a given set of facts, to tests of memory, and to the instrumental skills that are supposed to demonstrate their competence. The purpose behind pupils' intelligence is clear; to understand themselves and people better. The purpose behind the school's demands is never clarified. It is assumed as if it were obvious. Whilst it does not strike pupils as having any real meaning, they extrapolate the idea that this is the way people have to be made to fit for employment.

    Every day, we witness the conflict between two forms of thinking, until one is suppressed for the sake of the other. Whilst it could be argued that the human spirit of exploration can never be wholly stifled, it does become diminished. The idea that life itself is for the sake of education, for learning, for satisfying curiosity, does not appear to be part of schooling.

2. Pupils learn that all questions are closed. It seems there are only right and wrong answers. They are not allowed to make mistakes. Getting the answer wrong is either reprehensible or humiliating.

    This means that intelligence is diverted into trying to guess what it is that the teacher wants them to say. Every dialogue is like a test. The teacher is seen as a holding the correct answers and pupils do well or badly by memorising what these are. Open questions, those which ask for an opinion or demand a logical reason, disappear. If the answer is already known, think the pupils, then why ask the question?

3. Pupils are burdened by the concept of memory of a certain kind. There is nothing more useful than to marshal evidence to support an argument. But this is where memory has a purpose, an outcome. When the facts become learned for their

own sake they lose much of their meaning. When they serve an argument, facts are associated with purpose – they become essential.

Much of pupils' experience centres on meaningless tasks; meaningless in the sense that there is no clear purpose for them, nothing that connects with their lives or the world outside school. Mechanical exercises, the rote learning of rules, remain a form of submission; to test and to reward or punish. Such a regime has no purpose beyond itself. What could be learned and remembered with ease becomes a chore.

4. Pupils become accustomed to low expectations. Much of their time is spent in carrying out routine exercises. They refer to this as 'doing things'. The notion of 'time on task' encapsulates this, the steady application of silent pupils in carrying out set work. Of course the work has to be of a presentable standard, and this means neat and tidy, but this cannot be in itself the ultimate purpose.

There are several pressures to maintain low standards. One is the conformity to the pace of the majority; not to stand out or upset the even flow of the steady progress of the whole class. Another is the demands of a large group of people to do the same thing at the same time, without distraction and without talking or exchanging ideas. Another is to produce a lot of work, to fill the pages, to copy out notes, to repeat work that has been done before. Another is to work to the standardised tests, to achieve particular grades in just two core subjects without any concern with other kinds of intellectual demand.

5. Pupils find it easy to give up trying. When they adapt to minimal requirements the very idea of intellectual ambition or excitement becomes laughingly distant. This does not mean that there is no pressure. The cajoling parents and the competitive nature of tests place a strong burden of expectation on the pupils. This is not the same as the demands of intelligence. They are the demands of performance and conformity.

The pressures on pupils to not really try are subtle. They insinuate themselves into the styles of thinking to which pupils become accustomed, the steady an undemanding routines, losing subtly the excitement that makes learning so pleasurable.

It does not have to be like this

*   Every pupil will have a personal interest that can be encouraged by finding out what it is and taking some time to develop it. Intelligent curiosity will not have been completely stifled.
*   Every pupil will have a favourite subject. It might not be maths or English but any subject that is pursued with interest has a positive effect on the rest.

- Every pupil learns as much by talking as by listening. Just as every teacher has a tendency to assert that they learn more than their pupils so is the need to explain to others a good way to learn. Talking is not all bad!
- Every pupil longs to have subject boundaries broken down. Every connection between one discipline and another brings not just extra associations, but makes intellectual sense.
- Every pupil wants to have his learning related to the real world. Every fact is more interesting if it can be applied to the world that pupils see around them, in their homes and neighbourhoods and through the media. Relevance is all.
- Every pupil loves stories. Every story and every anecdote gives vitality to facts. Personal experience brings to life otherwise dry material. And personal interests make teachers interesting.
- Every pupil is interested in debate and controversy. There are many issues that can be discussed. There will be opinions about them even if half formed, or even when there are no particular opinion an awareness of the issues. Debate allows for tolerance, respect for different opinions, open questions and intelligent independence.

Seven principles to apply

1. *Why?* 'Why' is not so much a principles is the one open question that should be employed wherever possible. It is the question that denotes intellectual respect, a genuine curiosity in the answer. It is the essential tool that needs to be used, replacing not just the words of signal and command like 'right' (the word most used by teachers). To invoke the word 'why' is to create situations in which it is useful. This means open-ended discussion, the employment of evidence and reason. It gives pupils a challenge, but it also expects them to be able to meet it.

   'Why?' is the beginning of all curiosity, the desire for answers to real questions. It is only by being used often and genuinely that the stranglehold of closed questions can be loosened. It suggests that pupils have opinions of their own and that they should be involved personally in their own learning.

2. *Logic.* Pupils possess an undiminished ability to employ critical thinking, to unpick an argument or question a statement. Wherever a course in philosophical thinking is introduced, it invariably demonstrates hidden talents in reasoning.

   Philosophy sounds like an arcane subject, but it goes closer to children's thinking than any other. It does not just provide answers but opens up possibilities. It is a way of thinking, a confidence in one's own intelligence. It demonstrates to every pupil the potential of the mind, the need for proof, as well as the playfulness of thinking.

The ability to employ critical thinking is the power of standing up for oneself intellectually, to have the confidence that everyone has a human right to think, rather than letting such a commodity lie unacknowledged or in abeyance. Any statements can be challenged. The result is a dialogue, an exchange of ideas rather than the reception of assertions, and the widening of curiosity in all kinds of ideas, whether they are good or bad.

3. *Games.* Playing intellectual games, which may seem trivial, is acknowledged as a useful exercise for the brain. Games can cover a range of subjects beyond the recall of facts. They can be mathematical or based on language, like crosswords. They can be as simple as lists or as complex as mathematical conundrums, but at best they give the sense of the pleasures of intellectual engagement. Games are not matters of passing the time, like reading a comic, although they are often used as time fillers. They are the small exercises that bring in extra interest and which have nothing to do with formal testing.

4. *Experiments, testing various hypotheses.* Pupils often have very interesting explanations for scientific phenomena, which are original, if wrong. By not giving closed answers and by allowing them to work out the solutions for themselves, pupils are encouraged to think and share their thinking with others.

   Experiments do not have to be elaborate. They can be as simple as testing how far different materials bounce, making sure the test is fair and, encouraging guessing as well as exploring explanations. Experiments deal, like philosophy, with logic, empirical evidence and reasons.

5. *Real life.* To pupils, schools are microcosm of society and they observe and learn all kinds of behaviour from established hierarchies of control to struggles for power. They base their understanding on how society operates on these experiences, and yet they do not see schools as being the 'real world'.

   Real life belongs elsewhere, with houses and homes and families, with neighbourhoods and television. Whilst some aspects of reality, like bad behaviour, confronts them violently in school, the formal curriculum seems like a system in itself, hermeneutic, cut-off and, to a large extent, unconnected to the rest of their lives.

   One of the reasons that the curriculum seems so lacking in purpose is that it makes few concessions to the questions people want answering. Whenever a connection is drawn in the formal curriculum to real events, actual social processes or real dilemmas there is an immediate benefit. All kinds of processes or skills of scientific principles or mathematical logic are brought to life.

   Pupils tend to keep the two worlds, their personal lives and the experience of school, apart, to the diminution of both. Making connections with reality involves all those intelligent attributions that are otherwise lost.

6. *Parody.* Parody is a way of learning. It includes modelling, trying to find out how others have done or understood things. It is not the same as imitation, since it is rare to perfectly emulate the exact counterfeit of other people.

Most creative artists learn by parody. They are strongly influenced by the cultural practices of others before they strike out on their own. They do not always realise that they are using parody, but when they do, they are aware that they are learning by seeing how other people have done things. Parody is a gift for all pupils. They enjoy all kinds of things from the trivial to the profound. Parody is a kind of homage to originality.

Parody also connects to the real world. Many school exercises have nothing to do with anything pupils will ever come across again. Let us take an example. Pupils are often asked to write a story. This is usually on one or two sides of A4 paper. The result is never satisfying. But where else, ever, does one come across a complete story in a few hundred words? It has nothing to do with what they will ever encounter again. It is, instead, far more efficient, more enjoyable and closer to the spirit of the original to ask them to write one page of a novel that happens to be on the opposite side of an illustration. Their parody then invokes all kinds of things, suggesting riches of plot and a sense of an ending.

This is just one example, shortly described. The principle it underlines is that parody is a way of looking at, and understanding, how and why people have presented material to each other, whether in the arts or sciences. Parody is the clue to analysis and far easier to do.

7. *Creativity.* This is not just a metaphor for all the alternatives to dull routines and mechanical testing. Creativity is hard work. It is practice and concentration. Any good or original idea needs work.

Creative hard work, however, involves the kinds of thinking that pupils bring with them to school. It has a sense of the audience, a real one and not just a test. It makes use of associations, exploring ideas. It knows that the presentation, the style, is at the core of the endeavour are not an afterthought to be 'done again'.

Creativity means having the interest and enthusiasm for a subject that sustains interest. It is not confined by fear of being wrong or afraid of criticism, but is carried out in the spirit of sharing understanding.

Conclusions

There are many natural connections that teachers have with pupils, and many artificial barriers that replace personal relationships. Recognising the intelligence of young people, believing in their possibility, itself makes a profound difference to them. Instead of confrontation and the clash of wills, of forcing compliance and asserting dominance, all of which are a waste of energy, there should be far more mutual interests despite all the barriers that educational systems appear to set up.

10

Relationships
What teachers need to know

Children have firm views about what makes a good teacher. The characteristics can be grouped under three headings: integrity, explanation and involvement. Each of these overlap and merge and make a coherent whole. It must, however, be stressed that these characteristics are not matters of personality. Good teachers are individuals, with their own style. I have had the privilege of observing hundreds of teachers, and am constantly amazed at the variety, as well as the emotional and intellectual subtlety of their performance, especially in the conditions in which they have to work.

Personalities vary, and one is often surprised by how one can never anticipate or guess who has that art of managing and stimulating a classroom. This is because it depends not on personal characteristics as much as on relationships. In their practised observations of teachers, pupils know exactly what these characteristics consist of:

1. *Integrity.* This is not an easy term to define, and there is a modern tendency to misuse the term, to change it into jargon, as with so many other words, to wash it clean of its real meaning. Integrity means being honest with oneself, taking account of evidence, but being loyal to decisions, being truthful and trustworthy. Together with understanding others (which implies more than tolerance) it leads to an acknowledgement of oneself and interest in and compassion for, as well as realism about human nature.

   There is nothing magical or erudite about integrity. It means simply doing one's best and doing so for other people. At the most simple level it means 'Do not try to be liked'.

   Yearning for approval, seeking to please, can be corrupting. Any susceptibility to flattery is undermining. Pupils' good relationships with their teachers depend on trust, that the teacher will be consistent and fair. In the case studies of teachers who have had disastrous effect on the pupils, it is clear that the reason for the mood swings is not simply self-indulgence, but insecurity, a sudden desire to be liked, and attempts to win over some sympathy.

He screams at you, and like afterwards, one of my friends got really upset. And he started like, being more friendly and saying. 'I'm your friend.' I don't think that's right. You go crawling back to a child after you've started at them just to become their friends. (girl, age 10)

Teachers are closely observed by pupils and their individual characteristics analysed and forgiven. Pupils make a distinction between individual personalities and the public behaviour on which they rely for rectitude and consistency. Ideally, the personality of the teacher with charm and humour goes together with this quality of fairness, but for pupils the common dominator is integrity. They want to know where they are with the teacher. They want to believe that he or she treats them all equally.

Teachers cannot do much about their personalities, but they can remember the basis of all real relationships, the honesty and the straightforwardness. All the teacher needs to do is to try, to achieve that security of knowing that the intentions are clear. Pupils do not expect miracles, but they do yearn to know how they stand. Relying on the teacher's fairness and consistency is an essential. As with the balance of good parenting, the teacher displays neither too much control, nor too much leniency.

The axiom for the teacher is to be yourself and concentrate on the role of good classroom organisation and fair personal relations. One should remember not to try to be popular by simply indulging. One could also remember that for the pupils the phrase that sticks out from the most difficult circumstances is the dread of being 'picked on'. This can be inadvertent, but it can also be avoided.

2. *Explaining.* This characteristic emerges from integrity. What pupils most appreciate from the teacher is caught by their use of the word 'explaining'. Explanation does not mean that the teacher knows everything, but that he has time to spend with individuals. She takes each request seriously and likes to work with pupils rather than against them. There is a fundamental difference between setting targets and testing whether the pupils are achieving them (with dire consequences to those who fail), and nurturing individual abilities and interests and encouraging them to find out things for themselves through a variety of sources.

One major source is the encouragement by the teacher. When pupils talk about 'explaining' they are encapsulating a major characteristic of relationships, of sharing intellectual curiosity and taking ideas seriously. 'Explaining' means as much listening as talking. It is diagnosing a problem, understanding the feelings of individuals, and quite simply, working with them.

To create the time for explanation means a well-run classroom where there is individual activity and collaboration. The pupils need to understand the rules of good conduct, not to interrupt, to accept the needs of others and acknowledge the limited time the teacher has.

The teacher who is characterised as being able to explain is actually the one who shows a willingness to listen, to take each individual seriously. She might not have time, but she makes it clear that she is always willing to help. Explaining is a type of relationship, rather than intellect. There is no threat, and no sense that they will be told they are stupid. Pupils quickly detect irritation of those teachers who feel that every request to help is an interruption or who tell pupils to keep themselves occupied with 'do it again'.

3. *Personal interest.* Integrity includes running a well-ordered classroom in which everyone knows what he or she is expected to do; explaining means taking individuals seriously. Personal interest means something more.

Pupils make it clear that they are interested in the individuality of teachers. They know that teachers have to play a role, and they are also aware of more complex backgrounds of personalities. Whilst the personality should not contaminate integrity, it is still a major interest.

Pupils also make it clear that they appreciate those times when they have individual conversations with shared interests and no official agenda. The memorable conversations are the unexpected ones, those that suddenly change the routines of duty and the syllabus. The other extreme of being 'picked on' is a genuine interest in the individual.

When teachers know this, they can make a point of making use of it. It is even possible to make use of two simple rules of thumb. If the teacher makes a point of giving a word of praise to every individual in the class at any opportunity, it makes a difference. Better still is the private individual word, remembering the detail or circumstance that can show that shared knowledge is not forgotten. Even in helping with an individual piece of work, it is worth noting something about it, to follow up to ask about it again. Such insight makes a difference, far greater than one small matter learned.

There is nothing worse than feeling ignored. Anthropologists have long noted the deleterious effects of feeling neglected or sidelined. It is the more negative equivalent to the feelings of envy, but it can be equally corrosive. In the hurly-burly of crowded classrooms, it is very easy for pupils to feel neglected. They are accustomed to neglect from some of their peers, but if it is an ostensible friend, that is a different matter. Most detrimental is neglect from the teacher.

Just as pupils point out that the beneficial effects of explaining, that practical personal interest, so they elaborate on all those periods in which they feel the teacher is indifferent to them. It could be that the teacher is too busy and does not want to be distracted, but the refusal to respond or show interest is taken personally. The kinds of phrases that keep returning in pupils accounts include:

Get on with it.

Go away.

She hasn't done anything about it.

I don't feel I could go to any teacher, if it was my own problem.

Come on, get on with that work.

Sit there and be quiet.

Paying attention to every individual, rather than telling them to get on with it is not easy, but necessary. This is a matter of willingness, rather than circumstance. The pupils are aware when teachers are willing to help even if they are busy. They resent the underlying indifference, which is based on being more interested in having a quiet classroom, with no interruptions, than pupils' individual progress.

This willingness has to be stressed, because the pupils detect this. The circumstances are unfavourable. There are so many individual needs, and the pressures of time. Ideally, one would change the circumstances, since the consequences of a sense of neglect and indifference can be significant. Meanwhile, any attempt to demonstrate interest in each pupil makes a difference.

There are practical things to be done. The shared running of the classroom with agreed types of conduct, gives time for other things. The beginning and end of the day, and of each lesson, is an opportunity for personal dialogue and individual enquiry. If the pupils always have something to do, to read and to enjoy, the teacher can make a point of talking to individuals. Having something special to talk about with each is a starting point to which each pupil will add. Often pupils do not expect personal interest. It is as if they invite a certain amount of indifference so they can be anonymous, if not invisible. Once they realise that their interest is reciprocated they will feel encouraged to pursue such conversations. Iterative dialogue should be the heart of the classroom.

Rules and collaborations

Having times for individuals depends on a well-run classroom. Classroom management is often depicted as a set of rules, of order and discipline. This might be true but all rules depend less on force than on agreement. One of the main relationships between teachers and pupils (and with each other) depends on the mutual shared understanding of conduct – what is expected and why.

Nothing is of greater interest to children than the way people behave with each other. When pupils learn to cope with school, they soon appreciate the difference between petty rules and matters of greater concern. They often feel that rules are arbitrary, imposed without any deeper rationality than teachers' whims. The sense of unfairness derives from this. At one level, rules are matters of organisation, of tidiness, of knowing where things are kept. At another, they are ways of creating order, or of imposing wills, as in the case of uniforms and conforming to a set of interpretative guidelines. The rules that engage children's support go deeper.

Agree on a shared plan. In all the work on children's rights and charters it is sensible to involve the voices of children themselves. The good running of the classroom depends on more than etiquette. It rests not just on agreement or compliance but on reasons. If pupils are involved in drawing up what is expected, in terms of good conduct, support and kindness, they are far more likely to bear them in mind and be more responsible towards each other outside the classroom. It is not unreasonable to expect pupils to understand the rationale for the codes of conduct: they will have sensible views. If they subscribe to what is reasonable, then there will not have to be a confrontation or the imposition of will. A sense of guilt or remorse will replace the anger or frustration of being 'picked on'.

Such rules of conduct should be pervasive, with expectations that cover all aspects of life in the playground, as well as the classroom. They should be constructive, rather than reactive.

Prevent bullying

A common complaint of pupils is not just the amount of bullying but the refusal of teachers to react to it. The response to this is to point out the lack of time, the difficulties of getting to the causes and effects and sorting out the details. The only way to deal with bullying in all its subtle forms is first to acknowledge its existence, or at least the possibility of its existence even when hidden, and anticipate it. This means having the collaboration of all pupils, so that they will help and no longer remain silent witnesses.

Dealing with bullying means concentrating on relationships as well as conduct, on understanding the causes and effects of teasing, undermining, ostracising as well as the pupils abusing each other physically or verbally. It is only when there are agreements on what is acceptable behaviour and what is not, that all the pupils will be involved. It also means that teachers stand a far better chance of having time, of being available, of being sympathetic, as well as being arbitrators.

Prevention and anticipation is better than reaction because it involves understanding the issues, the temptations and the causes. Rather than campaigns against certain problems like bullying there should be concerns for positive conduct. The rhetoric of political correctness might be pervasive, but does little to improve people's conduct.

Keep instructions to a minimum

If rules are worth while, they need to be understood and acted on. In pupils' experience of school, they hear a great deal of meaningless noise in the form of directions towards an individual that all hear. They learn to stop listening. The constant cajoling, the invocations to keep quiet, with each repetition getting louder and louder, is not just a distraction but reinforces the sense of meaningless and ineffective control.

Much of the background noise of school sounds as if it belongs to the pupils but each real conversation could be full of meaning. It is possible to have a crowded space like a restaurant where people talk quietly. The sensitivity to other people is usually matched by courtesy in the conversations. If pupils talk to each other with meaning, with a dialogue that is more than a simple enquiry or expletive, that is of a different order, as is such a dialogue with the teacher.

The languages of classroom instruction are pointed out by pupils as being of a particular type, but they are the words of interference, of essential powerlessness, of loss of control. The explanations for good conduct and the agreement to abide by them should be so firmly established that they do not need constant reminders or repetitions.

Make relationships central to the curriculum

The time that is spent on establishing the rules of good conduct are not just an elaborate way of enforcing discipline. They go to the heart of children's interests, puzzlements and enquiry. The question they keep asking themselves is why people behave the way they do.

The formal curriculum has all kinds of manifestations in which certain concepts predominate:

- a separation of subjects, of different fields of knowledge.;
- the significance of mechanical skills, of rote learning and carrying out routines;.
- the weight of facts to be remembered.

None of these things are imbued with a purpose. There might be reasons for the curriculum that pupils guess at, like preparation for employment, but they do not touch on pupils' own interests. These remain intact in the hidden curriculum, all that takes place outside the boundaries of subjects.

The main purpose of education should be understanding. People can't survive without it. Whilst policies place education at the centre of making more money and improving competitiveness, the interests of most people who consider themselves educated, lie in the excitement of discovery, in learning something new and understanding. If this seems completely obvious, it should make one pause. It is very little to do with policy or with the education system as it is run. It might be the implicit intention of teachers, the development of every pupil in the extension of personal learning, but this is separate from what pupils take as the explicit purpose of school.

The teacher's personal concerns are often at loggerheads with the system; the pupils' concerns are close to the teachers'.

If the centre of the curriculum is with the understanding of human conduct this would give meaning to all the pupils' work. It is the concern of history, geography and philosophy as well as other subjects. Those scientific subjects that seem most distant from humanistic concerns are nevertheless driven by them. Once pupils have a core of understanding, which includes the question 'why?' all the other activities they undertake, however peripheral, will be given more meaning.

The focus of human behaviour means attention paid to society, to politics, to business, to the environment, to globalisation, and to all those matters that are the centre of curiosity and of communication. We make jokes about grumpy old men because they are no longer distracted by their personal career from asking why things should be as they are (or why they are so bad). This sense of bewilderment comes out of open exploratory questions about human behaviour. This 'grumpiness' is shared by young children who want so many questions answered. By looking at the nature of relationships they are connected to what they see taking place around them and to their observations of each other.

Relationships with the disaffected

When one considers the reasons for the disaffected, one can understand why personal relationships are so important. Amongst the causes of disaffection are:

- isolation
- disillusionment
- boredom
- gangs
- misunderstanding roles.

The sense of isolation is felt by everyone sometimes, but affects some deeply. As in the experience of young children, neglect is resented. Whilst many try to keep a low profile, this is because of the fear of making relationships. Isolation is a personal reaction as well as an external event. The inability to hold onto a trusting relationship has all kinds of long-term causes. Many antisocial behaviours, whether mild or extreme, derive from feeling isolated, outside the events that matter, and disconnected from others.

Disillusionment is a sense of social and personal disappointment. It is social because of the constant comparisons with others, driven by envy. The sense of general unfairness is fed by resentment with all the extreme contrasts between people. It includes a feeling of not knowing why some should be so lucky. This leads to the human characteristic of blaming oneself. The sense of envy of others, a resentment at success, is fuelled by the sense of personal inferiority and inflamed by unfairness. It makes the person feel like an outsider, isolated and neglected.

Boredom is the public version of what some psychiatrists call 'normlessness'. In public people talk of disaffected youths, having nothing particular to do, needing to be distracted from themselves. This sense of purposelessness is not the same as the daily boredom of carrying out routines, of passing time in trivial entertainment. It is a feeling of meaninglessness, of not having a purpose or real sense of personal identity. It is a purposelessness very easily led into temptation.

Gangs provide the distractions that the lonely seek, because they offer an alternative to normal relationships. When an individual is insecure and uncertain, the easiest way to acquire a sense of identity is to be defined against others. Standing out against some others, being seen as different, is an aggressive way of being noticed, even resented. Wearing certain kinds of clothes is the most obvious way of drawing attention by giving offence, by demanding and then resenting other people's reactions.

But such gestures are never carried out in isolation. They need others of like mind; they need an audience. The gang is a type of audience. There is rarely meaningful discussion. Instead of a relationship which depends on arguments and understanding, definitions and agreements, gangs provide the option of a kind of friendship without demands, approval without insight, even admiration without basis.

Pupils will show off, can be those 'jokers' who know just how far to go, who cause laughter to be inclusive. They can also be those who want to draw attention to themselves and prefer to be laughed at, rather than not noticed. They crave some kind of notice even if this is not approval.

In the absence of normal, complicated even difficult relationships, gangs are presented with the conditions in which to form.

Misunderstanding roles

One of the main causes of actual exclusion is the final outburst when, after a history of truancy and disaffection, a pupil will lose his temper and turn on a teacher. This often comes about because the teacher has insisted on a demand to which the pupil refuses to comply. The pupil takes the teacher's reaction as a personal affront.

The problem is that the pupil has misunderstood the differences between role and personality.

Pupils accept that the personality of the teacher is enshrined in the need to carry out a role. They know that there will be possibilities of being reprimanded, but they also know this will cause no lasting resentment. When the disaffected find themselves in difficulties with authority they take it personally. This is as if the policeman, fulfilling a function, were felt to be holding a personal grudge. This is the bewilderment of the insecure mind that tries to take offence whenever possible, that turns every transaction into the brutally personal.

Such mistakes are another side of the failure to understand relationships. They also reiterate how important it is for teachers to attempt to create good individual relationships. Nevertheless, in the prevailing conditions, teachers will be confronted with the aggressive, the suspicious and the resentful and have to deal with them. Knowing the causes is important, but there are three ground rules which help:

1. *Avoid battles of wills.* Given the propensity of the difficult pupils to take things personally there is no point in sheer force. Besides, in this climate of blame, the teacher would receive no support, certainly less than the aggressor. Once the role of authority is no longer believed in there is no use in attempting it. This, however, is the opposite of suggesting that nothing should be done. On the contrary, the teacher needs to demonstrate interest by pursuing the matter by trying to find the cause so it can be dealt with. There are many diverting things to do; but the central message the difficult pupil receives is that what he does will not be ignored, partly because it is not right, and partly because he still matters. He does not have to be an outsider.

2. *Leave no one out.* It is too easy (and understandable), to be utterly relieved when a more difficult pupil fails to appear at the start of the day or lesson. It is also easy to hope that he will remain quiet and out of sight. This is simply a way of passing on problems to others. Every connection of a personal kind can do more good than one imagines. Every pupil will have interests, even if nefarious, so it is always possible to show some curiosity. It does not matter if the subject is a far cry from one's own tastes; the fact of personal interest is important.

   One reason for the significance in the teacher's interests, however fleeting or symbolic, is because it is disinterested. We are not paid to be social workers or mentors. In that role of personal interest teachers become an individual. The role is then the person.

3. *Prevent the formation of gangs.* The stress on individuals includes personal relationships but should also resist the alternative. It is much harder to deal with group mentality, with the gang and their audience, than with one pupil. The people who need dealing with are in fact, the onlookers, the encouragers, the witnesses, all those who secretly enjoy the discomfiture of others. All teachers

have seen the relish of watching others get into trouble. There is no pity or mercy in that feeling. This is why it is important that the whole class discusses social issues and helps deal with them.

Relationships with peers

The relationships that pupils have with each other should not be a different world, a separate experience from the mainstream school. What peers learn from each other should be made central. The range of subjects learned from each other is vast if unofficial. It includes some formal elements of the curriculum, but the real sense of interest lies in two other matters: relationships and external events.

The relationships about which pupils talk are not only those with each other or those they observe taking place with teachers and peer groups but those witnessed in society. These external events are not neutral items of news but symbols of people's behaviour. This is the central subject of the external sources of information.

Pupils like talking to each other. This might sound like chatter, rather than 'time on task' and can be a distraction. This can also be used. Pupils learn by teaching. They learn with each other. Constructive group work, meaning pupils being asked to collaborate instead of merely sitting together, works in a way that not only makes sense to them but is analogous with the way they will work in real life in the future.

The principle of asking open questions should be joined by making sure pupils have lengthy and constructive conversations with each other. It is part of the discovery of learning and of learning through discovery. The fact that pupils enjoy talking should not make it forbidden.

In a famous experiment on class sizes in the United States it was found that the most effective intervention depended on pupils helping each other. This proved more beneficial than reducing the class size or by introducing new teachers. The only other successful way of promoting learning is to ask some expert who is not a teacher, and who has a varied interest, from skydiving to surfing, to come and give a talk. The relationship is then of shared curiosity, not the formal imposition of what should be learnt. Relationships, seen as a subject as well as a technique, should be the centre of the curriculum.

11

Sources of information
Implications for teachers

Broad and balanced?

The one statement of principle that is made about the National Curriculum is that it should be 'broad and balanced'. Nothing is said of aims or purposes, let alone values. As long as the curriculum covers a wide range of subjects, that is supposed to be enough.

Nothing could contrast more with the curriculum derived from other sources. Some of the differences are extremely significant. The curricula of the home, the neighbourhood and the media are of immediacy and relevance. It is opinionated, as well as political. It depends on attitudes, on gossip, and on scepticism. It is influential without being sacrosanct.

The formal curriculum of school actually eschews and avoids what it sees as contamination by the reality of life. It rests on the accumulation of facts, the memorising of significant details like dates, and the implementation of skills and rote learning. It presents itself as having the strength of neutrality, of the avoidance of opinions or contradictions. It cannot help being received as monumentally dull as a whole.

Whilst pupils know they have to accept the curriculum as a given and learn to assume that it is the academic that ought to be taken seriously, there are two consequences:

1. They look at other sources of information, like politics and international events, as ephemera, not to be taken seriously. The basis of opinions on fact is forgotten, and the wide-ranging images accepted as superficial. This does not help a balanced view of the world.

2. A whole source of learning is made little use of. Opinions matter. They should
    be based on broad knowledge. They are not just judgements made for effect on
    the spur of the moment. They are influential.

What is lacking in the formal curriculum is relevance to the real world. What
is lacking in other sources of information is the pursuit of true judgement and
understanding, weighing the evidence, learning what can be trusted. The clash of
two types of knowledge has fatal consequences for both.

Teachers have a role in putting this right, in applying academic standards of
empiricism to the everyday and making the curriculum exciting and relevant. The
problem with the formal curriculum is that it is often superficial. The problem with
other sources of information is that they are taken superficially.

Attempts to cover vast swathes of knowledge for the sake of fulfilling the
requirements of targets, rather than for a deeper purpose, mean that there is a danger
of all being viewed as having no depth. Prejudices are nearly always based on ill-
informed or badly digested information. It is easy to fall into an attitude which
sees all things in similar terms if there is no real understanding of the context of
knowledge. This is why purpose, having a clear vision of why things need to be
understood, is so important.

Just as the background noises of collective work and constant reminders of
discipline go over the heads of pupils, so do all the accumulated facts and tables
pass them by. Those moments of disillusioned boredom come when pupils
are supposed to know things they find irrelevant to them. Mixed with their
disappointment of their own performance comes the bewilderment of what these
things are for, wondering why they have to know a times table or the correct
synonym or translation.

The irony is that the sense of covering the whole of the curriculum, with being an
all-rounder, that ideal that marries a love of literature with excitement at the second
law of thermodynamics, is quickly undermined by the higher ideals of universities.
There, specialism is all. Distinctions of subjects are replaced by subject boundaries.
Knowing one field in depth is considered to be more important than breadth. It is
also considered to be better for the skills of thinking. Knowing a subject really well,
so there can be informed discussion and disagreement, is seen as more civilising and
enlightened than piles of information.

At the heart of this debate between all-round awareness and study in depth is the
question of relevance. Whatever is undertaken needs to be done with conviction and
interest. It does not matter what the subject is. What matters is the way it is pursued,
and the encouragement that goes with it.

Either/or?

We should try to overcome the separation of different kinds of knowledge. These different kinds of knowledge do not consist of subject matter – the arts versus the sciences – but different ways of treating knowledge.

We need to know how to engage the pupils' interest. To this end, we have to understand what it is they want to know. How often do we ask them? How often do we engage them in contemplating the sense of purpose and relevance? Personal interests are important, but mostly latent. Pupils will always have two matters that interest them:

1. *A personal hobby, something they enjoy and feel they know about.* It does not matter what it is but it is important to connect it to the rest of their learning. We need to find out what it is.
2. *The sense of the meaning of the world and their place in it.* That is where watching the news, talking to their friends, experiencing the neighbourhoods and discussing entertainments are important. Everyone has personal interests to the extent of observing people, having opinions about them, and comparing their reactions to those of others.

Pupils rarely have opportunities to discuss the purpose of the curriculum. They are rarely encouraged to enjoy learning for its own sake, as they do in a personal interest or hobby. The contrast between two different types of learning is reinforced.

Pursue matters of interest

We cannot assume that everything is of equal interest, even if the National Curriculum asserts it. One can only learn to interest oneself in a subject if one has experienced the excitement aroused by interest. This stimulation does not mean withdrawal from other subjects but a renewal of hope.

Teachers should pursue three different kinds of interest:

1. *Their own.* It is only by revealing personal enthusiasm that the idea of intellectual engagement is clear. Pupils are stimulated by sharing a teacher's excitement for something which evolves from pleasure. This is why inviting anyone to share personal knowledge is so effective. And this is why the best remembered teachers of those who share their personal enthusiasm.

2. *That of the pupils.* All of them will have some kind of hobby, some accumulation of knowledge, even if it is of a football team. And all of them will have favourite topics on television programmes or stories.
3. *The shared environment.* Social issues are at the forefront of children's consciousness. It is always a surprise that matters of common interest, like politics and the political system, are left out of the curriculum. Real life and its understanding and contemplation, gives meaning to studying.

All people have opinions, but many are denied the proper engagement with the facts. People have an interest in events, an interest mostly ignored until they are disillusioned or prejudiced. Such an interest should be encouraged before this happens, whether the event is something on the news, especially a matter which affects everyone, or a topic of general discussion. Using such an item as a starting point, almost any subject can be made to become relevant. Such interest is the best starting point for the pursuit of a discipline, knowing it is relevant aids concentration and the determination to understand.

At the heart of such a discussion is the central question about people, their place in society, their motivations and their well-being. The ethical and philosophical approach is not oblique but central.

Concepts of identity

Values are at the heart of any learning. This is not because we ought to be moral, and contemplate existence in a certain light. It is because values are at the heart of children's curiosity. It is the first subject that interests them, the difference in people, and in their behaviour, the motivations of actions and the personalities that are brought to bear on conduct.

Morality is not a separate or imposed issue. It is not a series of doctrines or commands, but a way of understanding behaviour, one's own as well as that of other people. It is the meaning that pupils want to understand.

This is not a matter of humanism or purely of the arts and humanities. The answers to the question 'why?' underlines every aspect of the curriculum. It might most often be asked of people's behaviour but it is the lynch-pin of all subjects, the pursuit of logic, of answers, of finding out the evidence.

Whether it is through the intense experience of the playground and friendships, or the casual attention to news bulletins, the same question remains fixed in the minds of pupils. Their anguished questions of fairness and equity are all driven by the frustration of not knowing why.

Values are not some extra that needs to be given like a dose of medicine to recalcitrant or unwilling pupils. When they talk of 'respect' they mean the word in a number of different ways. It means an assertion of self-respect, of identity, of understanding relationships. 'Respect' might be understood as an ethically neutral term but it goes to the heart of the matter. Is respect a proper recognition of authority or is it the powerful authorities' recognition of individual human rights?

When pupils want 'respect' they want their questions taken seriously and their involvement welcomed. The disaffected are those to whom the information is never explained, and the purposes never outlined. They are left uninvolved until they demand some notice through confrontation. The notion of 'respect', usually associated with the disaffected of the belligerent, demonstrates how central is the concern with individual values and with relationships.

Knowing one's place?

Children's neutrality is a way of understanding themselves in relation to others. They have no deep-seated sense of superiority or of being especially blessed. Nor do they feel at first any strong prejudice against difference. Their snobberies are learned. Those biases are cleverly introduced to them. The very fact that they know contrasts between extremes in which they invariably see themselves in the middle can be an advantage.

The discussion of the world nowadays will always have an international dimension. The pupils themselves might be aware of their particular circumstances and care most about those things close to home but they understand the context. They are not parochial. They realise that there are major issues that affect all people.

Globalisation is about culture as much as it is about economics and the environment. There are material issues that affect all. Such concerns should not be ignored as a waste of time or as an impediment to the delivery of the curriculum. Without such issues the curriculum is dead.

Explore sources of information

In addition to the school as a source of information, with its teachers and library, pupils are increasingly aware of the other types and styles of communication. Some of these can be exploited formally, like all the information accessed by computer. They can also be opened up at home with a whole range of outlets, of opinions, of facts and exemplars.

This demands some discrimination. Not all sources of information are reliable. Whereas at school the pupils tend to treat all facts at the same level in a bland acceptance – and indifference – the information that they receive on the Internet can be superficial as well as knowledgeable, as biased as it can be fair.

Pupils need to know how to analyse information. Nothing is clearer than the contrasts between accounts in different media to the same item of news. These differences of opinion can be exploited, for they can teach pupils to discriminate and analyse. They should not just accept a bold statement of fact or be influenced by an overheard remark. They need to know the constraints imposed by time as well as interpretation, by the uses of 'gloss' and 'spin' (or plain lies). Thus, the question of what they gleaned from last night's news which happens to interest them is also a signal to each other on the ways in which people will interpret and present ideas.

Looking at other sources of information outside the school is a reminder of the volatility, as well as the excitement, of subject matter. It teaches a greater respect for empirical data with a more profound sense of relevance. Asking what interests them, or what they learned the night before, is not a way of passing time but a means, a starting point for critical analysis.

The analysis of information

The quality of information is not as important as the quality of its interpretation. Despite what might sound like sacrilege to some people, interpretation and discrimination are significant. There is still a tendency to want to impose censorship, to make sure that pupils receive only such material as is deemed worthy. Such concern can run to preciousness. More important is the ability to compare, to discriminate and to make judgements.

Pupils have a wide range of private interests, including the pleasure of reading. It does not matter if they read what are popular pot boilers, like many best sellers. It is the way that they learn to read them that counts. Just as looking at a television show can be done in a vacuum of inattention or with critical analysis, so can any material be interpreted. Indeed, the more crass the material scrutinised the easier it is to form a judgement about it.

The skills of developing argument and explaining a judgement are to be fostered. They are real skills, not mechanical exercises carried out for their own sake, but the application and nurturing of opinions resting on fact and capable of being defended or amended through argument. The skills of reading or looking at pictures or weighing evidence are all at the service of something worthwhile.

Rather than view with disapproval young people's interest in the most popular authors, it is better to encourage them to understand how their work is constructed, what makes it popular and interesting. Most adults can read novels with pleasure whilst knowing they are tosh. What children need to learn is discrimination and judgement. Just as they see the ways in which facts are presented through the different media so they can understand the manipulations of the audience through style.

Style or self-parody?

The word 'style' conjures up for many a sense of sophistication or superiority. It is often considered the last bastion of taste or discrimination. It should be the first since everyone is aware of it. Whilst allowing for the fact that everyone prefers some things to others, and will have their own sense of vulgarity, the concept of 'style' simply means being aware of the medium as well as the message. The ability to understand how prose is written and what effects are being made, comes as naturally to young children as seeing others' points of view. They see in people the different ways in which they are presented with truth and falsehood, or simply a bias. This applies to all kinds of secondary forms of communication. It is a sense of distinction that should not be lost.

If pupils are aware of style, an awareness that needs encouragement, they are not always blessed with the ability to explain their point of view. This is where parody is helpful. It is simpler to 'take off' an act than it is to analyse it. The essentials are understood before the vocabulary if found.

Applying criticism and judgement is a way of giving confidence in opinions, since one might vehemently disagree, knowing one's own impeccable taste, and yet there is no right or wrong. These are open questions applied to a wide range of information.

There is real intellectual pleasure in challenging information. Knowing that all forms of communication are a form of construction, and understanding the difficulty in getting them right the first time, is an encouragement to understanding not just style but what the content means. Comparisons between different ways of presenting the same thing help form judgements. Such analysis can be carried out on any type of material. All can have their own opinions and learn how to present them.

Collecting information

Pupils like ownership of material if that means that they are accumulating it for themselves. They like lists. Some people continue to enjoy making collections and such acquisitiveness is at the heart of all discrimination. An expert in a subject accumulates information but he does so because he wants to, not because he must be prepared to be tested.

As with hobbies, collecting information, like objects, can be fun. Lists encourage organising abilities as well as discrimination and pupils derive pleasure from their stimulation of the thought. They are like a mental exercise or puzzle. They are a way of giving everyone a sense of pleasure in facts. They also give a sense of personal ownership.

What is it all for?

The sources of information referred to here are all manifestations of the actual world, not the microcosm of school, not the version of events proffered in the National Curriculum. They are the stuff of passion and involvement, and the centre of interest and curiosity. The 'grumpy young people' look at the world like 'grumpy old men' asking why things are as they are. Between those times people spend their time busy with work, with getting on with the more immediate distractions of life.

Such questioning is also an engagement with the world, a sign of curiosity and interest. Whilst pupils suppose their rite of schooling is a preparation for their futures, through qualifications ultimately to employment, they often fail to see how this can be so, except for the fact that exams count. They do not really see the purpose.

When employers are asked for their opinions they often lament the lack of talent in the young. They regret their lack of willingness to learn, to engage with others, to understand communication. Universities similarly lament the lack of cultural awareness in their intakes, the lack of a critical edge, of interests and social knowledge. Something is lacking in the National Curriculum. There are ways of mitigating its failure if not putting all completely right.

12

How teachers survive

The use of the term 'survival' must seem odd. It is how the new teacher feels confronted by a difficult class. Simply to survive is not enough. Teaching is only a joy when all the energy is directed to the pupil's progress and the shared understandings of discovery. It is when the teacher is also learning and redefining ideas that simple survival is put aside. It is nevertheless a useful term to describe the position that teachers find themselves in, not in relation to their pupils, but to their place in the system.

The term 'survival' suggests that the role of the teacher is undermined by constant demands and by complex distractions. It puts the teacher in a defensive position as if coping, the use of survival strategies, the concern just to remain in office, was paramount. For those teachers who really care this is what it can feel like. There are people entering the profession who see it as their way of pursuing private enterprise, as if schools had become small businesses – a way of making money – but this is a vision of the system that cannot last. It is possible to do perfectly well by adapting to being a part of the teaching system but it is important to be aware of all the different dangers of forming such a perspective on teaching. The irony is that such a different approach to survival would work better in a different type of system than the one we have now.

Meanwhile, the first point to remember is that in the real education of individuals, in the whole scope of learning, teachers, those who try to help, play the most crucial and important role, despite managerialism. No teacher is ever fully aware of all the good that he or she has done. The very fact that there has been a motivation to help others, to make the world a better place, means that the effects are often immeasurable. They are usually unseen and only, when it is too late, do individuals remember the effect of teachers who fitted their role to their own learning needs. The problem is not just that people are ungrateful but that they are unaware.

The first way to survive is to enjoy as much as possible of all the learning that goes into teaching. In the balance between the professional and personal, the personal is often underrated. The teacher has to find things that are of real interest. These are usually in a subject, in reading, and in sharing with others the pleasures of discovery. Enjoyment is crucial. It is also something that has to be learnt since real pleasures are also demanding ones, rather than matters of passing the time in distraction. This is one of the main things that teachers should be instilling in their pupils. There should be no dichotomy between learning and pleasure. Once they become opposites, both suffer.

Looking for those moments that are most enjoyable is an important theme, and the teacher needs to have a wide range of interests of his of her own. This is the positive side and carries over into the next means of survival, which is to understand what is not satisfactory in the system rather than accept it as it is. One is in a far more positive position when one is able to do what is important, whatever the context. There will always be people who will support the true teacher. Teachers tend, as good head teachers point out, to submit too readily to the demands of others. Teachers do not have to follow all orders in the way in which they are laid down. A teacher should not do what is not seen to be right, or which makes one feel uncomfortable. One can get away with a great deal; so the weight of new policies and instructions should not simply be adhered to if they do not make sense. Often they do not make sense, or are contradicted by successive weights of legislation. A healthy scepticism is helpful. Knowing that the newest of ideas are often repetitions of what has been invented several times before makes the need to follow one's own path more clear.

Teachers do not have to collude in absurdities of pretensions or camouflage what they do. They do not have to take statutory demands too seriously. A teacher has to stay with what he or she is best at and avoid those who try to undermine. A well-run school, with teachers supporting each other and having a clear idea of their own integrity, might be seen as 'maverick' but it will be successful and respected for pursuing what is best.

The third way of surviving is to enlist support from fellow teachers. There might seem to be absurd demands by inspectors and others, but these can be by-passed if one has the confidence of one's fellow teachers. To do this means sharing values and working collegially with others. It cannot be stressed enough how important it is that teachers feel that they are doing something worth while. There is a lot of professional expertise involved and, much more important than that, there is an expertise in learning, in caring, in having wider concerns than the simply instrumental. Teachers know that what they are doing works despite the system. To ignore or undermine the system they need as much support from each other as possible and this, of course, involves all those who are related to or part of a school.

The contrast between the instrumental and the far more complex realities of learning are encapsulated by the way in which the word 'creativity' has become used as a symbol of defiance against a purely target-ridden agenda. Creativity does not actually mean what it pretends to mean and has much more to do with spontaneity. Nevertheless, it has become a symbol for dealing with learning in a way that is quite different from inspectorial and measurable norms.

All those worthwhile activities that pupils learn from have a sense of purpose and a sense of discovery about the real world. There is nothing that contrasts more with thick mechanical exercises of tests than the pursuit of understanding. The philosophical debates, the controversies, the real questions of the time, a sense of trying to find meaning, all are part of the purpose of learning.

True learning is lost once it is deprived of its intention to be a collective as well as a private experience that includes like-minded people. The pupils constantly remind us of the routines, the purely mechanical exercises of the kind that are dull, meaningless and undemanding. The pupils do not simply suffer from boredom but feel undermined by the experience when the whole purpose of learning is lost. By the end, managing a class is not a matter of coping but a matter of helping the pupils learn in their own way.

The real secret is that if a teacher has a genuine interest of her own she will be in a position to respond to what excites the pupils. The irony is that the pupils desire to come to a teacher, to find somebody to respond to their interests and to help them with their own questions. Pupils should be at the centre of the process. They are the ones who need teachers. The teachers are approached as those who have their own interests, their own ideas, not because of what they ought to be teaching but because their awareness stimulates their own understanding of the world. When the balance is right between teachers and pupils the learning process becomes comfortable for all. The present circumstances, let alone the basic structures that have been the same for many years, do not help this. It is the role of the teacher to get the better of the circumstances until such a time with the whole education system is transformed.

What to promote

Success in teaching lies in several factors which cannot simply made into a formula. This is why so many of the promotional books, or the leadership manuals, can be so unsatisfactory. They seem to forget that individual human beings are involved, that relationships are not based on command and subservience. Success lies in having both the conviction in what one is doing and feeling that there are colleagues who have the same outlook and who are willing to support. One cannot simply fit into a team without thinking, so personal integrity is vital, but it is important not to feel isolated, out on a limb, the only person doing what is 'right'.

One principle is a disinterested concern for the pupils – 'disinterested', the opposite of uninterested. It means being concerned for them for their own sake rather than the satisfaction of personal success, or for outcomes that please those in power. This concern for other people is one that remains constant, is calm and curious, and not an intense scrutiny of all that they do.

The other principle is that of engagement; being willing to be involved, not to be indifferent to what goes on. What is out of sight should not be out of mind. Engaging with the interests of the pupils, their conduct and attitudes to each other, should be constant. In the end this gives more space for the teacher, even if it sometimes feels that we wish to escape to the staffroom, rather than have all of one's energy taken up in the ceaseless struggle. The pupils quickly detect when the teachers would prefer not to be there; they know the psychology of relief at not having to be responsible.

These two attitudes of engagement and disinterested concern are in a fine balance; they are not contradictory nor are they the same. Teachers will recognise the psychological state involved. It is not a deliberate stance but the kind of attitude that shows that the teacher is unafraid, is involved, is unselfconscious, but has the integrity to be committed, without being emotionally entangled. It is something that can only be learned by action and attitude.

What to avoid

There are two essential problems with the ethos of schools, and the pupils are concerned with both of them. The first is the sense that all kinds of things can take place and remain hidden; not only undetected but ignored. There is a whole world of interactions and alternative social learning that takes place outside the normal structure of the lessons, and this is not really a 'hidden' curriculum. It is an essential part of school, for good or bad, and if ignored, then it is the latter.

Pupils resent the indifference that seems to be expressed towards their own problems, the internecine strife, all those matters that can make school life miserable. Bullying is a persistent problem and one which is ubiquitous. Bullying is a complex phenomenon in which all are involved. Even if not perpetuating some cruelty of the tongue, and even if not an obvious victim, all are involved as witness and spectators.

The deepest moral dilemma does not concern the small number of unpleasant and bullying individuals, but the bystanders that not only let it happen, but by doing so find a secret satisfaction that it is happening to someone else. When a whole society is twisted into the worst excesses of bad behaviour, it is because the majority remain silent, and try to be hidden. The playground is a place of learning about society, and it is not a bad analogy of what can go wrong. The real problem is the deliberate ignorance, the lack of moral courage that allows the victims to suffer, even if their suffering is not relished. In any good society, the individual voice matters as does not allowing the wicked to get away with it. Being neutral or passive is a moral failure.

The second matter to avoid stems inevitably from the conditions of indifference and passivity. It is the rise of a kind of tribalism, of the dominance of groups. This can happen in the staffroom as much as the playground, when there are coteries of insiders and outsiders, favourites and those to be subtly anathematised. The 'balkanisation' of a school into factions can happen too easily and the results are disastrous.

In the psychology of discipline the avoidance of gangs, and the confrontations with groups is central. All depends on the ability to deal with individuals, one at a time, rather than a collective. The same is true of the more subtle psychology of the institution as a whole. It can be undermined if the sense of individual worth and collective enterprise, in which everyone is individually involved, begins to break down into factions. What pupils most fear is that there are dominant groups that begin to dictate attitudes that isolate the well meaning and the hard working. They can create a counterculture that undermines the ethos of learning. The attractions of the tribe are obvious, the creation of the favoured few and the defining of opposition. What is less obvious is how often this can happen in schools.

Striving for position is an essential human characteristic. Just like a pack of dogs, there will be a desire to find out which is most powerful, who is top dog. With animals, such struggles are everyday and immediate; with people it is more subtle, but there is still an element in any competitive circumstance. It the intense atmosphere of university, for example, placing of oneself against others – who will get a first?; will they be successful?; do they have enough limitations to do really well? – pervade the subconscious of many. The same sniffing and manoeuvring takes place in all institutions and needs to be recognised as destructive.

The teachers' involvement and engagement is necessary because there is always a temptation to let things carry on as along as there is no obvious disturbance, and as long as it is out of sight. The problem is that the corrupting influences abound and become the formative influences in the society of the future. The system has a lot to answer for.

What to remember

There are four crucial factors about the education of pupils that teachers should always bear in mind. A constant reminder of these not only helps us but comforts us. It reminds us that we do much more good (or harm) than is immediately apparent, and that we are not to be made instantly culpable for all that goes wrong.

1. The first factor is the intelligence of the pupils, an intelligence that in terms of brain power is formed early. It therefore needs to be helped and directed.

Pupils are not simply passive and indifferent receivers of an official curriculum. They have their own powerful concerns and seek to find answers to the basic questions that affect all. Some might try to stop all thinking and involvement, but this is not possible. Every pupil has a brain.

2.   The second factor is the sources of information. These are not controlled by the school but are derived from a range of elements – from the media to peers. The kind of knowledge that people have varies as much as their attitudes and needs to be nurtured, for the big questions of human behaviour, of politics and international relations are not part of the official remit of schools.

3.   The third element is the vulnerability of the pupils to all kinds of influences, many of them hidden. The emotional stress that people feel, through teasing and by way of overheard remarks, should not be underestimated. This is as true, of course, of the staff as the pupils. The sense of being undermined, of not being highly rated, of being disparaged or an outsider, is one that all teachers will recognise, not only in their own memories of schooling but in their teaching experience.

4.   The fourth factor is the importance of relationships and this is the heart of the learning experience, and therefore of teaching. The individual dialogue, the shared interest, the mutual understanding – all depends on that. The successful system promotes all the opportunities possible for such an iterative engagement. It is through the pleasure of the teacher that the pupil redefines the learning experience. It could not be more unlike the regime of schooling but that is what teachers have to contend with.

The basic message, again

The most important weapon a teacher has is the essential truth about teaching and the education system. Most people are concerned about the times they live in. They can either say that people will always be as they are, including the wicked, as if there were nothing that could be done about it, or they can rail against or be puzzled about the iniquity and injustice because they do not feel this is inevitable.

Understanding that the way people behave depends on upbringing is crucial for teachers. There is no excuse for ignoring the importance of the environment. All the latest genetic research shows how central (like language) is the way in which the young are brought up. The essential problem is that the education system does not address it. When we consider what the young most want to understand, and when we acknowledge their response to their circumstances, we know the crucial part played, negatively as well as positively by schools.

Anyone who wishes to find answers about behaviour and society will look at the educational experiences, but those in power then make a fatal mistake. Knowing that it is not working leads them to blame those involved rather than questioning the fundamental principles. Teachers must know that the faults are not theirs but are of the system. It is only teachers who mitigate the worst aspects as best as they can.

This stance is a positive one that explains the difficulties sensitive teachers face and gives them the courage of their convictions. The research evidence on cognition and through the insights of pupils is overwhelming and something ought to be done about it. Meanwhile the teachers are the ones who are, despite all the odds, doing more good than they know.

- People count, not systems. Systems, after all, depend on people but they depend on people thinking of themselves as merely part of a system. The best and essential part of education lies in the individual learning. Each of us knows this. It is part of our experience as individual human beings. But the system is based on alternative principles of manipulation, targets and accountability and the kinds of outcomes that are not hopeful to learning. It is a puzzle how things went so wrong. Society, and the communities that make it up, is more than a system. Learning is social rather than an imposed system.
- If individuals count then there must be a belief in all pupils or what are teachers for? The teacher does not want to be likened to a gaoler or an inspector, the seeker of blame or punishment. The teacher is an enabler rather than an imposer and that highlights the juxtaposition between the essentials of teaching and the system.
- There must also be a belief in learning. If the teacher is not learning and taking pleasure in it, then that sense that the pupils detect, that education matters, is lost for them and lost also are the outcomes of learning: curiosity, the ability to know oneself, good conduct and understanding of others.
- All this amounts simply to integrity, being oneself and the upholding of values. That is all the counts. It is not onerous, but neither is it simple in the conditions of a flawed system of education.

References

Alexander, R. (2000) *Culture and Pedagogy: International Comparisons in Primary Education.* Oxford: Blackwell.

Aries, P. (1962) *Centuries of Childhood.* New York: Knopf.

Armstrong, A. (2006) *Children Writing Stories.* Maidenhead: Open University Press.

Becher, T. and Trowler, P. (2001) *Academic Tribes and Territories.* Buckingham: Open University Press.

Besag, V. (1989) *Bullies and Victims in Schools.* Milton Keynes: Open University Press.

Bloom, P. (2004) *Descartes' Baby: How Child Development Explains What Makes us Human.* London: Heinemann.

Bowles, S. and Gintis, H. (1976) *Schooling in Capitalist America.* New York: Basic Books.

Burke, C. and Grosvenor, I. (2003) *The School I'd Like: Children and Young Peoples' Reflections on an Education for the 21st Century.* London: Routledge.

Cullingford, C. (1991) *The Inner World of the School: Children's Ideas About Schools.* London: Cassell.

—— (1992) *Children and Society: Children's Attitudes to Politics and Power* London: Cassell.

—— (1996) *Parents, Education and the State.* Aldershot: Ashgate.

—— (1999) *The Causes of Exclusion: Home, School and the Development of Young Criminals.* London: Kogan Page.

—— (2000) *Prejudice: From Individual Identity to Nationalism.* London: Kogan Page.

—— (2002) *The Best Years of Their Lives? Pupils' Experiences of School.* London: Kogan Page.

—— (2007) *Childhood. The Inside Story: Hearing Children's Voices.* Newcastle: Cambridge Scholars Publications.

—— (2008) *How Pupils Cope with School.* Newcastle: Cambridge Scholars Publications.

Cullingford, C. and Haq, N. (2009) *Computers, Schools and Students: The Effects of Technology.* Aldershot: Ashgate.

Damasio, A. (2000) *The Feeling of What Happens: Body, Emotion and the Making of Consciousness.* London: Heinemann.

—— (2003) *Looking for Spinoza: Joy, Sorrow, and the Feeling Brain.* London: Heinemann.

Davies, L. (2003) *Education and Conflict: Complexity and Chaos.* London: Routledge.

Day, C. (2004) *A Passion for Teaching.* London: Routledge.

Day, C., Kington, A., Stobart, G. and Sammons, P. (2006) The personal and professional lives of teachers: stable and unstable identities. *British Educational Research Journal.* Vol. 32, No. 4, pp. 601–16.

Dennet, D. (2003) *Freedom Evolves.* London: Allen Lane.

Dickens, C. (1865) *Our Mutual Friend.* Dent: Everyman Library.

Donaldson, M. (1993) *Human Minds: An Exploration.* London: Penguin.

Dunn, J. (1988) *The Beginnings of Social Understanding*. Oxford: Blackwell.

Egan, K. (1997) *The Educated Mind: How Cognitive Tools Shape our Understanding*. Chicago, IL: University of Chicago Press.

—— (2002) *Getting it Wrong from the Beginning: Our Progressivist Inheritance from Herbert Spencer, John Dewey, and Jean Piaget*. London: Yale University Press.

Elias, N. (1982) *The Civilising Process: State Formation and Civilisations*. Oxford: Blackwell.

Eliot, G. (1872) *Middlemarch*. London: Penguin.

Elliot, J. (1998) *The Curriculum Experiment*. Milton Keynes: Open University Press.

Ferneyhough, C. (2008) *The Baby in the Mirror: A Child's World From Birth to Three*. London: Granta.

Harlen, W. (1985) *Teaching and Learning in Primary Science*. London: Harper and Row.

Harris, J. (1998) *The Nurture Assumption*. London: Bloomsbury.

Heath, S. B. (1983) *Ways with Words: Language, Life and Work in Communities and Classrooms*. New York: Cambridge University Press.

James, W. (1890) *The Principles of Psychology*. New York: H. Holt.

King, R. (1978) *All Things Bright and Beautiful? Sociological Study of Infants' Classrooms*. Chichester: John Wiley & Sons.

Measor, L. and Woods, P. (1984) *Changing Schools: Pupils' Perspectives on Transfer to a Comprehensive*. Milton Keynes: Open University Press.

Mortimore, P., Sammons, P., Stoll, L., Lewis, D. and Ecob, R. (1979) *School Matters: The Early Years*. London: Open Books.

Pinker, S. (1997) *How the Mind Works*. London: Allen Lane.

—— (2007) *The Stuff of Thought: Language as a Window into Human Nature*. London: Allen Lane.

Pollard, A., Triggs, P., Broadfoot, P., McNess, E. and Osborn, M. (2000) *What Pupils Say: Changing Policy and Practice in Primary Education*. London: Continuum.

Pye, J. (1989) *Invisible Children: Who are the Real Losers at School?* Oxford: Oxford University Press.

Quinn, V. (1997) *Critical Thinking in Young Minds*. London: David Fulton.

Reddy, V. (2008) *How Infants Know Minds*. Cambridge, MA: Harvard University Press.

Richman, N., Stevenson, J. and Graham, P. (1982) *Pre-school to School: A Behavioural Study*. London: Academic Press.

Robertson, R. (2006) Managers, middle managers and classroom teachers; a study of secondary schools. Doctoral thesis, University of Huddersfield.

Rose, S. (2005) *The 21st Century Brain: Explaining, Mending and Manipulating the Mind*. London: Jonathan Cape.

Rutter, M. (2005) *Genes and Behaviour: Nature–Nurture Interplay Explained*. Oxford: Blackwell.

Rutter, M., Maugham, B., Mortimore, P. and Ousten, J. (1979) *Fifteen Thousand Hours- Secondary Schools and Their Effects on Children*. London: Open Books.

Schoen, D. (1987) *Educating the Reflective Practitioner*. San Francisco, CA: Jossey Bass.

Ulrich, W. (1996) Politicians and parents. In C. Cullingford (ed.) *Parents, Education and the State*. Aldershot: Ashgate.

Wells, G. (1985) *Language Development in the Pre-school Years*. Cambridge: Cambridge University Press.

Winkley, D. (1999) An examination of Ofsted. In C. Cullingford (ed.) *An Inspector Calls*. London: Kogan Page.

Woods, A. (1996) School initiatives with parents. In C. Cullingford (ed.) *Parents, Education and the State*. Aldershot: Ashgate.

Woods, P. (1990) *The Happiest Days? How Pupils Cope with School*. London: Falmer.

Woods, P. and Jeffrey, B. (2002) The reconstruction of primary teachers' identities. *British Journal of Sociology of Education*. Vol. 23, No. 1, pp. 89–106.

Index